W0006860

Praise for *touched*

"Brave. Powerful. Vulnerable. Truth-telling. Desperately needed silence breaking. Wise and practical guidance. These are only a few of the ways to describe the awe-inspiring gift that Shanell T. Smith has given to all of us—survivors, caregivers, and all people of faith—who want to learn how to more effectively address and actually stop the rampant sexual violence perpetrated by church leaders and the complicity of church folks who willfully sacrifice the victimized to protect the perpetrators."
—**Traci C. West, author** of *Solidarity and Defiant Spirituality: Africana Lessons on Racism, Religion, and Ending Gender Violence*

"Shanell Smith guides readers on a soulful journey through the spiritual abuse church folk inflict when they silence, shame, and ignore survivors. But she does not leave us there. On she leads—down that slow, hard, but life-giving road to hope. To healing. To being better—for survivors, for ourselves."
—**Linda Kay Klein, author** of *Pure: Inside the Evangelical Movement that Shamed a Generation of Young Women and How I Broke Free*, **and founder of Break Free Together**

"Shanell Smith's book is profound, significant, troubling, difficult, and deeply faithful. Smith writes with characteristic practical and profound passion. She tells a candid story about the church and sexual assault—a story filled with practical wisdom for both survivors and those who love them. *Touched* is powerful realness and practical wisdom for anyone touched by sexual assault."
—**Katherine A. Shaner, Wake Forest University, School of Divinity**

"*Touched* is a transformative volume that professional caregivers desperately need. Shanell Smith has provided a life-giving gift for wounded healers with a desire to help and not further harm those who find their way to us. The wisdom within these pages are a must read for people of faith in the age of #MeToo."
—**Shelley D. Best, President & CEO The Conference of Churches and The 224 EcoSpace of Hartford, Connecticut**

"In *Touched*, Dr. Shanell Smith confronts the ruthless rape culture that exists within the Church and addresses the cultural layers of shaming and silencing that challenge the ability of survivors to overcome sexual trauma. She rightly indicts the church for its role in perpetuating the normativity of violence against women and protection of predators. She powerfully anchors this book in the telling of her own story, thereby modeling the concept of "sounding the alarm" that she articulates in the book. She goes on to provide practical instructions for survivors who are seeking holistic healing, through various stages of coping, healing, truth-telling, and ultimately, healing.

Smith also provides guidance to church leaders who desire to be better equipped to walk survivors through journeys of healing through the lens of faith. Smith has created an invaluable resource for survivors of sexual assault, and for Christian pastoral care providers to survivors. This is a necessary addition to the library of anyone who is ready to do the work of redeeming the soul of the Church from the lasting effects of sexualized violence."
—**Neichelle R. Guidry, Dean of Sisters Chapel and Director of the WISDOM Center, Spelman College**

touched

touched

For Survivors of Sexual Assault Like Me
Who Have Been Hurt by Church Folk
and for Those Who Will Care

Shanell T. Smith

Fortress Press

Minneapolis

TOUCHED

For Survivors of Sexual Assault Like Me Who Have Been Hurt by Church Folk and for Those Who Will Care

Copyright © 2020 Fortress Press, an imprint of 1517 Media. All rights reserved. Except for brief quotations in critical articles or reviews, no part of this book may be reproduced in any manner without prior written permission from the publisher. Email copyright@1517.media or write to Permissions, Fortress Press, PO Box 1209, Minneapolis, MN 55440-1209.

Cover image: "Dual Ladies" by Anthony Armstrong. Used by permission.

Cover design: Laurie Ingram

Print ISBN: 978-1-5064-4815-2

eBook ISBN: 978-1-5064-4816-9

Dedicated to fellow survivors and those who will care for them.

Contents

Introduction

he touched me
HE TOUCHED ME!
A supposed man of God,
a Bible teacher, pulpit preacher
laying hands on you
while he preys
on you.
he touched me.
in a way i will never forget
in a way i wouldn't dare let . . .
i still feel dirty.
clear waters return murky.
why did he hurt me?
did I tell him to stop?
how far did it go?
was I roofied when it happened?
because I do not know
how it ended.
i just remember being home.
oh God, what else did he do
when he had me alone?
i sounded the alarm . . .
twenty years later, i did,
because all that time
my brain hid the trauma
to protect me from going insane.
as i saw him each Sunday

raising his hand in praise.
i could not have handled it,
i would not have survived.
my brain locked up my trauma
to keep me alive,
and i am thankful.
but twenty years later
when it was released
my brain flooded with images.
i was no longer at peace.
i needed to tell someone
what he did to me
and i did.
as a daughter of the church
i did what i knew.
i went to church leaders
and some folk in the pews,
but they did not help me.
i thought that i knew
them.
but they silenced me
said the most hurtful things,
dismissive, accusatory,
unsettling things,
and i thought they had wings.
self-doubt and blame sank in
because i went to them.
they had the power to protect,
power to correct wrongs.
what happened to God's justice
we sang in those songs?
God's agents?
yeah right!
they imparted nothing but
more hurt when they denied
me.
the foundation of my trust
was rocked
not only in church folk but also in God.
God's not
who i thought God was.

everything got mixed up,
God's people with God's love.
my assailant, the folk at the altar,
those i sought help from
there would be no help
but probably laughter
when i left.
after i told them
i felt bereft.
human error
led to church terror.
he touched me.
i told them he hurt me.
why did God desert me?
leaving me with church folk
who had failed me.
they *did* nothing
but they *said* everything
they should not have.
things that retraumatized me,
things that did nothing but silence me,
to hush my horror
to smother the sound of my screams.
as if i suddenly was profane
they turned me away
in Jesus's name
and it nearly destroyed me.
nearly.
because i am still here
and i am strong!
i found other folk
to encourage me along
my journey
toward healing.
my form of healing
which is not a destination.
it is a moment-to-moment excursion,
a self-love expedition.
i am unlearning what they taught me
i am witnessing God as Love
and i am sharing my truth with each of you

so that you can rise above
whatever others use to hold you down.
i want to help build you up,
i want you to get the help you need
so i am giving you something from which to learn:
ME.
here, i tell *my* truth.
here, i affirm *yours*.
hear, O caregivers, what to do and say
when a survivor comes knocking on your door.
may each of you learn from my experience.
take what you need and leave the rest
and as you journey toward healing.
do what makes you feel good,
nothing more, nothing less.
permission has been granted.
feel what you feel
do what you need to do
love on yourself
be fierce!
i offer solidarity,
encouragement
and hope, to name a few.
please accept what i offer
because i offer you, YOU.

Touched is part memoir, part instruction. It is based on my own traumatic experience with sexual violence and the lack of support and care I received in a church setting. I am writing from *my* perspective as a Christian, but this book is still beneficial for those of different faiths.

This book is a work of intense vulnerability. My purpose in writing this is twofold: to affirm the stories of other survivors and to offer some directives for those from whom they will seek support and care. I would even suggest that my fellow survivors give this book to those with whom they are considering sharing their stories. Reading this book ahead of your conversation may act in a preventative fashion; at the least, your caregiver will have a head start in how to listen to you and ultimately care for you.

He touched me. Inappropriately.

I was sexually abused by a church leader as I discerned my call to ministry. He *touched* me as I was seeking to be touched by the Spirit. He *used* my body as I sought to be used by God and God's ministry. As I write this, I still cannot believe that it happened to me.

While my sexual trauma did not occur *in the church building*, a male leader *of the church* did it. Then, those *in the church* to whom I "sounded the alarm" did nothing. When one church leader did nothing, I went to another, and then another. I experienced intensifying subsequent sexual trauma as I told and retold my truth to those I thought would support me, and more important, do something!

In my experience, the church plays a major role in my trauma not only because of my assailant's leadership position in the church but also because of the church leaders I went to for support. I must note, however, that the phrase "in the church" does not necessitate that the sexual offense strictly occurs in a church building, during a church event, or in the physical confines of church settings. "In the church" includes those who are sexually violated by a member, even a leader, of the church community, but in a different physical location, as in my case. "In the church" includes those who seek help from those who work or worship within the church. Even more important, however, "in the church" refers to survivors who believe in God and who, because of their sexual trauma, experience a strained or broken relationship with God *whether or not they belong to a church community*.

Nevertheless, my work is not just for believers. Each chapter can function as a standalone chapter and does not solely provide directives for believers. It just so happens that the context of most of my encounters that I include occur within the church walls or with church folk. They are still people, people who say the wrong things, and inflict further pain on survivors. That can be anyone.

Throughout my book, you will also find that I use the gender-neutral, nonbinary third-person singular pronouns *they, their,* and *them.* Gender inclusivity is very important to me, and so I want to honor that.

When I initially began writing this book, I used the word *caretaker.* When a mentor of mine mentioned this term as we talked about my work, a lightbulb went off. The mentor noted that the term *caretaker* sounds much more abrasive and not as soothing as *caregiver.* As a survivor, I am tired of folks *taking* from me. As I approached individuals seeking care and support, I wanted them to freely *give* it from their hearts. So *caregiver* it is!

I employ the term *caregiver* to refer to the person to whom we "sound the alarm." I make the assumptions that a caregiver can have two basic functions: to provide support and/or to seek justice. These two roles do not always overlap. The person to whom you "sound the alarm" is not necessarily the same person from whom you will seek personal support and care. They may be an authority figure who can seek justice on your behalf, make charges, arrests, remove an assailant from (ecclesial) office or leadership positions, and so on. A certified therapist, professor, and officer of the law are a few examples. This person may not comfort you, tell you that they will be with you every step of the way, offer a shoulder for you to cry on, and so on. It is important to know this. The caregiver to whom you "sound the alarm" may not be in the position to provide both justice and supportive care.

A final point of clarification that is warranted is my use of the phrase "church leader." In this book, "church leader" refers to folks in leadership positions (pastors, elders, deacons, stewards, etc.). I understand that there is a marked distinction between those roles. The pastor may be the head of staff and the face of the church, while the others support that leader in that role. Any church leader, however, who proclaims the Word of God may be understood as the voice of God. Church leaders can also be referred to as representatives of God. This notion can compound the trauma of a survivor who is also a believer, especially if their assailant is a church leader. This is because the boundaries between the profane and the sacred can become blurred. As you will see, this can lead to a strained or broken relationship between a survivor and God.

Power is usually shared among church leaders in varying degrees. Each leader has some capacity to seek justice for a survivor who has "sounded the alarm" by having tough conversations and interventions, making decisions, and enforcing policy in their church.

I intentionally do not employ the distinction between pastors and church leaders for two reasons: (1) to protect the identity of the "church leader" whom I went for comfort and (2) because the advice that I offer in this book is not determined by one's position in the church. Every "church leader" has the responsibility to *do something* even if all they can do is refer (see chap. 5).

A "man of God" touched me. Inappropriately. And God and God's people did nothing.

I did not "sound the alarm" until almost twenty years after my sexual assault occurred. As I later explain, my brain had compartmentalized my pain in order to protect me. When my brain thought I was safe, which just so happened to be when I moved to a different state, parts of my trauma were released. When I "sounded the alarm," I was an ordained clergywoman, a professor of New Testament and Christian origins, and a wife and mother of two boys.

When I "sounded the alarm" to several leaders of a church, I was retraumatized due to the lack of support and blatant dismissal I received. The church, for me, became a place of terror. The line between the church and my relationship with God was blurred. The church, I came to realize, was the devil's playground. I was duped! I was angry. Heck, I still am. Although it was "church folk" who hurt me both physically and emotionally, I also felt that God hurt me too. God let me down. God did not protect me.

As a person of faith, sexual assault, especially by a church leader, resulted in me distancing myself from God. I felt abandoned by God because of the actions of one who was a representative of God. I hated God. God hurt me. God left me to fend for myself among wolves in sheep's clothing. Questions of theodicy, that is, why bad things happen to good people, continue to plague me. "If God is all powerful, then why . . . ? If God is all knowing, then how come . . . ?"

The carnal and the spiritual became blurred. The boundaries between the earthly, spiritual connection with church folk and my spiritual connection with the divine became permeable. And when those boundaries were violated, the result was catastrophic. I could no longer separate God from God's people. I still cannot. Nor could I see the church as a safe space. It still is not. The church, the building itself and the people who worship within its walls, is no longer a place where I can find God. But in the church, I did find a predator. Or better yet, he found me. I did find church leaders and laypeople who did not come to my aid or do anything when I shared my truth.

Sexual violence "in the church" in all the ways described above crosses the boundary of the flesh and penetrates the spiritual realm in a violent fashion. It is catastrophic. It is life shattering.

It is a daily struggle. My relationship with God is not as strong as it used to be, but it is on the mend. One moment at a time. I am trying my best to see church folks as imperfect beings and to differentiate them from a loving God. Church pastors and leaders are human, and they will fall short of our expectations. The line between God and God's people is beginning to become clear again.

I am grateful for the wisdom of spiritual and professional mentors. Because of them, I am able to share with you the importance of telling your truth. Talk about your sexual trauma and your resulting pain and wavering faith. Be open about it. Not only will you be true to yourself, but you will also model that truth for other survivors and caregivers.

This book does *not* guarantee that if you follow my instructions, you will never experience a lack of support. My hope is that you can share this book as a resource for potential caregivers. I am not an expert on sexual violence and healing. I am not a therapist. What I am is a clergywoman who experienced sexual assault "in the church" and who was emotionally and spiritually scarred from the lack of support I received.

It was necessary to take pen to paper and share my truth not only for my own healing but also to show solidarity with other survivors who may have experienced something similar and as a way to validate their stories, their truths. I also seek to provide guidance to those who may be approached by a person who has experienced sexual trauma and who needs help in its various forms.

As a survivor of sexualized trauma, I am all too aware of the effects of viewing and touching. Voyeurism is real. Being the subject of another's gaze is unsettling. Being seen in this way can be experienced as touch. Thus I will not retraumatize myself or cause you to relive your own trauma by sharing all the details of mine. I share the context and conversation in which the response I received took place. The horrific details are not necessary for the purposes of this book. Nor am I open to or interested in hearing or discussing whether you would believe me.

What I offer is not expertise on the subject but rather reflective processing in a form of lament and prose that is based on my own sexual trauma. I offer my experience, from which I am hoping both survivors and caregivers will learn.

I have approached the writing of this book and the layout of each chapter as a trained Bible scholar. We exegete primary texts. We pick them apart. We determine what the text means, why it is being said, and for whom.

Each chapter begins with my primary text, that is, my own experience. I kept a journal. I saved all the text messages from the various conversations I had, and thus most of what you find here is what happened verbatim. Remembering is painful. I am grateful for my family and friends who provided comfort to me via letters, messages, and hugs.

After that, I speak to my fellow survivors. I am aware of the #MeToo movement first used by Tarana Burke, an African American civil rights activist, to raise awareness about the prevalence of sexual assault and sexual abuse in society. Although I do not engage this movement in my work since my experiences occur prior to the genesis of it, it is worthy of note and praise.

I include my analysis of sexualized trauma as a collective experience. This does not mean that our stories are uniform.

It does not mean that I understand what fellow survivors have gone through. Rather, I attempt to think beyond my trauma and imagine what others *may have* experienced or heard. ("Your truth *may have* entailed . . ."; "You *may have* heard . . .") My intent is to provide a window for what others have experienced. Like a fingerprint, each of our experiences is unique.

I also include an analysis of the responses I received to justify, relegate, or deny my traumatic experience. It is a *complete* list in my account, but by no means is it an *exhaustive* list in the general sense. You may have heard other hurtful things. The purpose of this analysis is not to excuse the people who said those things but rather to try to understand the source of such reactions *for me*. It helped me to consider the notions of power and authority and that perhaps they sought to have power over me because of the loss of their own sense of power. Perhaps there is more going on *inside* these individuals than what came *out* of their mouths.

Lastly, I speak to caregivers. After you've read what I went through, I want to encourage you to think on it. What does reading or hearing about a person's sexualized trauma do to you? How do you feel? What is your knee-jerk reaction? Does it take you to a bad time in your own life? What resources do you have at your disposal? Will you be brave enough to implement any tough measures? These questions and more will be asked in order to help caregivers think intentionally and strategically about the measures they will take should they be asked for help.

Writing *touched* was not easy, but it proved to be somewhat cathartic. I felt the trauma in the pit of my stomach like a heavy rock. It made me physically sick. I needed to release it. I am not healed. I have not completely moved on. I have not forgotten. I have not forgiven. For these reasons, I do not speak about forgiveness or reconciliation. I am not there. I do not know when or if I will ever be. But at this moment, I am happy because my trauma no longer lives inside of me as an *acute* pain, though there are still tremors.

Touched is not an academic book, although I am a scholar.

It does not offer medical advice (other than getting a therapist!), although I am a doctor.

What it offers is me—my truth, my experience, and my reflection on it all.

This piece, originally done with ink and colored pencil, perfectly depicts my feelings and the underlying emotional current of the content of this book. I am so grateful for her blessed artistic ability.

—Artist Magdalena Grabber. Remember her name.

(A link to the full color version of this image is available at fortresspress.com/touched)

1

IT IS NOT YOUR FAULT!

This chapter begins with me looking back at my experience. It tells the ways in which self-doubt and self-blame became my way of thinking. You may have gone through the same retrospective process. Initially I called this chapter "Ripe for the Taking," and then I called it "Retrospection Is a B*tch." But then I realized that I had fallen into the trap of that erred thinking. As survivors, we may replay what happened to us over and over in our minds, but I know one thing is true: IT IS NOT OUR FAULT!

My Trauma Begins

"Thank you for letting me try out my new massage oils on you." My neck jerked back because, you see, I had never said that he could do this.

I would have never guessed how my life would have changed after hearing those thirteen words. Thirteen words uttered by a man who I trusted wholeheartedly. Thirteen words from a God-fearing man. (Yeah right!) Thirteen words from someone who played a major role in my life and my transition from youth to adulthood. Thirteen words from a man that I would continue to see read Scripture and preach every Sunday and be an "uncle" to many youth, especially young girls without a father figure at home. *Hmm.* Retrospection is enlightening.

I thirsted for a father figure after my biological father left when I was eight years old. I yearned to be anybody's "little girl," since I could not be "Daddy's little girl," no matter how hard I tried. And I had tried. I was the "good girl." I did not get into trouble. I followed all the rules. My mother told me that soon after my biological father left, I said to her, "Don't worry, Mom, I'm gonna get good grades so that you will be proud of me." This is what I *said,* but what I *meant* was, "Don't worry, Mom, I'm gonna get good grades so that you *won't leave me too.*" I would do anything to make sure no one else I loved would leave me. I was the poster child for abandonment issues. If I am honest, and I might as well be since I am exposing all kinds of stuff about myself in this book, being the "good girl" meant not disappointing folk so they would never leave me. It is still my automatic reaction. I have learned, however, how to adjust my actions and reactions within the first few minutes.

I did things for others at my own expense. All. The. Time. What I wanted did not matter. *You want the last piece of cake? Take it. You want to be the soloist for that song on youth Sunday, even though you know that I practiced it for weeks? Ugh! Fine.*

There is always next time, right? I wanted that cake! I earned that solo! And yet I relented. I gave in. I did not put up a fight. Little did those people know that *they owed me* now. They owed me their loyalty. I was collecting friendships. I was racking up shores of love. Yeah. They can't leave me now.

Give, and they stay. Be good, and they will love you forever.

I suffered so that others did not have to, even if they were in the wrong. I always took the high road. This did not mean that I did not get angry. I just did it alone. I wrote about my experiences in my diaries. However, I was never explicit about my feelings—especially the "bad" ones—even in my diaries. *Oh my gosh! What would happen if someone found them? All those people! Too many people would have reason to leave me! I cannot let that happen. No. It won't happen.*

I needed *fatherly* attention, love, and direction. This is what I craved, although this need influenced my behavior toward *all* people. My deep desire for connection, affirmation, and approval from my father became a void that I would continually fail to fill. Nothing that I did made it better—from good grades to selfish acts of kindness. (Notice that I say "selfish" and not "selfless," because I always had ulterior motives: love and loyalty.)

That void would never be filled until I learned to love myself as I am, until I believed that I am enough. I didn't *then,* but I do *now.* One of my many therapists, a wonderful, Spirit-filled woman, once told me that I totally jack up the

"Golden Rule": "In everything do to others as you would have them do to you" (Matt 7:12 NRSV). Instead I acted as if it said, "In everything do to others *because you want* them to do for you." I followed that rule exactly, but in an unhealthy way. I held others to a standard that I expected—no, internally *demanded*—that they live by. Each time someone failed to meet God's expectation (read: *my* expectation), I would not view it as their own shortcomings but rather a deficiency in me. *What did I say or do? How can I make it better? Why don't you like me?! I did everything right!* I had to unlearn this behavior. I also had to come to terms with the fact that some folks will not like you for breathing.

I was the "good girl," the one who behaved the way everyone expected, with over-the-top, you-need-some-therapy issues. And I put this all on glorious display every Sunday, in my Sunday best. And he worked his magic.

He did not have to work hard. *Hey, Shanell. You look nice in that outfit.* (Compliment.) *You got a very good report card. Well done!* (Praise.) *Here's twenty dollars for your pocket. Go ask your mom if it is okay if you keep it.* (Gift and maternal trust.) *You preached very well. I know God is proud of you and your calling.* (Spiritual affirmation.) *Don't call him back. I know it's hard, but wait it out. He will call.* (Dating advice.) *Guess what? I'm taking you to a show for your high school graduation!* (Celebration and quality time.)

He provided everything that I wanted from my biological father. He earned my trust (and that of my mother). He praised me for my accomplishments. Helped me negotiate relationships. Assisted with, and encouraged me, to write and self-publish my first devotional, *Today's Prayer,* which led to *Today's Prayer, Volume 2.* He. Was. There. He was always there. Filling the gap. At least that is what I thought he was doing. But he was taking his time as he was biding his time. Digging in and taking root.

I imagine him watching me from afar before he worked his way in—into my extended family (where he is still welcomed, since many still do not know what he did to me), into my life (where he no longer has a place), and into my relationship with God (where my sexual trauma caused a great chasm to deepen).

He nourished our relationship until I was ripe for the taking.

Then he took.

It would be twenty years later when those thirteen words would return to haunt me, live and in Technicolor. I do not recall anything that may have triggered the replaying of my assault. I just remember the shock to my system. My mind protected me until I moved out of state, and the chances of my running into him were zero. When my mind felt I was safe, it opened up, and I remembered as if it happened the day before.

Day of Remembrance

On the "Day of Remembrance," June 29, 2014, I decided that if I had to relive this, so would he. So I quickly grabbed my phone, and at 9:10 a.m. I began to type out everything that I remembered so that he could remember what he did to me. (Yes, I still have the text conversation.) Did he think that I was okay with it after all these years? Did he think that it would never resurface? Probably. But not that day.

That day he relived it.

I could not think about whether he would "get off" from the retelling of what he did to me. I was hurting and angry, and I needed to express that to him. I needed him to know that I remembered. I wanted him to stir, wondering what I would do. I almost included the text message in this book verbatim, but as I explained earlier, I chose not to include *all* the details of my assault.

Our dialogue, which included a few back-and-forth text messages, ended that same morning at 10:34 a.m. with him saying, "If you ever want to talk about it or know what was going on with me during that time. Let me know. It was a dark time for me as my actions showed. Anything I can do to give you clearer understanding, answer any questions that you have. Just anything."

Really?! Dark place? Was he lonely in darkness? Was he saying he needed company, *my* company, in the darkness with him? A clearer understanding? Understanding?! There was nothing he could say to justify or explain his actions. Simply put: He was wrong! Thus my response to his message was, "It will not make it okay. No thanks!" This conversation left me bristling with anger. I was shaking. It was the first time I had talked to him as my assailant. It was unsettling, to say the least. But I am so proud of myself for doing it.

I did not understand how I was able to forget my sexual trauma for all of those years. In therapy I learned that oftentimes when we experience trauma, our brains shut down and go into protection mode. It was like my brain said, "We interrupt this programming . . ." Hearing this phrase was never a good thing. Good news almost never followed it. For my younger readers, imagine watching a video on YouTube, Netflix, or Hulu, and then the internet connection is lost. No one likes their favorite show—or one's life—intruded upon.

I remember shivering, shaking. I was ashamed, embarrassed, sad, and incensed! After reliving my sexual trauma from all of those years ago and this (insert the worst adjective you can think of) text conversation, I realized that something had to be done. Something had to be said. He was still an active church leader. And there were still fatherless girls in his midst.

It was high time that I "sounded the alarm."

So I did.

I would have never guessed that the alarm I tripped would be a silent one.

Seeking Clarity

Clarity in hindsight is sometimes overrated, especially when your retrospection results in blaming yourself for what happened to you.

Perhaps, like me, you asked yourself if you were "ripe for the taking." Were you an easy target? Did you know this person? Were you primed? Did your assailant take time to gain your trust? Did you belong to the same faith community? Did they work their way into your life, slowly but surely? Did they provide you with gifts? Did they praise you for your accomplishments? Did they offer their expertise and assistance to help you succeed in your career? Did they remark on how well you dressed or how good your hair looked? Did they say you were growing up to be a beautiful individual? Did they know that inside you were an emotional wound that you tried endlessly to heal? Did they attempt to be your savior? Were they your confidante? Were they there for you in a mentoring capacity? A spiritual advisor? Did they provide comfort for you in your time of need? Did they tell you that they love you?

Self-doubt and disappointment barged in. Are you kicking yourself for not seeing the signs? For not paying more attention to your surroundings? For being weak-minded? For not screaming louder? For not saying anything? These questions, and the answers to them, do not matter because OUR SEXUAL TRAUMA IS NOT OUR FAULT!

The reason I asked the particular questions above is because these were the ones that come to mind when I reflect on my history with my assailant. I could answer each and every one of the aforementioned questions in the affirmative. I have gone through each encounter that I could recall having with him with a fine-toothed comb. I questioned his motives, and I critiqued my acquiescence. I trusted him wholeheartedly. He could do no wrong. His advice was sound and solid. He had my best interest at heart, right?

Looking back kept me from moving forward. I blamed myself for something I should not have. I questioned myself: How did I not see this? Looking back, I cringe at how I did not pick up on anything. How could I not tell the type of person he was? (What are the signs of a sexual predator?) How could I not see that while he "mentored" all the youth, he paid particular interest in the girls, especially the fatherless girls? How did I not see this?!

Like a mother reprimanding a child, my therapist told me, "Stop! Just stop it! It was not your fault!"

She said that I have to cut myself some slack. I was young, trusting, and impressionable. I longed for fatherly attention, and he provided that for me. I welcomed it. There is nothing wrong with that. She did not help me come up with excuses. These are not excuses. These are facts. The bottom line is that I was living my life, and he took advantage of my situation. He was wrong. There was nothing about me or what I did to welcome that assault. The deceit does not lie with me.

Some may say that there is good and bad in everyone. I believe that. But in retrospect, I cannot see anything he did for me as good. I see it all as manipulation.

He invested. In me. And then he collected. From me.

It was not my fault!

My therapist helped me see this. She made me tell myself this every day.

As I wrote this chapter, I stirred in my seat and made disgusting faces to myself (well, to my computer) wondering how and why I felt compelled to be that "good girl," the one who never disappoints or toes the line. I wondered why no one saw that I was trying to fill a void and that I needed someone to whom I could talk about these feelings. Perhaps I hid them well. Too well, in fact. I got angry thinking about all of the things he said and did for me, thinking that they were from a pure heart. And perhaps some of them were, but in retrospect, they tell a totally different narrative. They tell a narrative of manipulative, predatory action. They show a tangled web of deception and deceit.

And then I remembered it was not my fault!

At first, I was so disappointed in my younger self. Despite going through many, many (*did I say many?*) therapy sessions, I found this difficult to let go. I want to go back to that little eight-year-old girl and save her. I wanted to snap her out of her delusion that love and loyalty can be bought. This, in fact, is one of the main reasons the people who I went to for help and support were able to hurt me so badly. While I want to say it is because they did not meet my expectations, the root cause of my disappointment and pain is because of my flawed understanding of what love truly was.

The way they responded to me is still not my fault.

I want to tell that little girl to *really* listen and absorb her mother's message and demonstration of authentic love and acceptance *just the way she is*. I want the opportunity to eat that slice of cake, to sing that solo, and to tell folks when they offended me and make *them* carry the burden of error instead of me. I want. I want. I want.

But I can't.

And it still is not my fault.

Dear Fellow Survivor . . .

They say hindsight is twenty twenty. That clarity can be both a good and bad thing. Negatively speaking, it can function as a source of self-blame. You may question yourself at every turn. In my experience, trust was present, and therefore vulnerability seemed safe. Perhaps it was the same for you. However, you may have been surprised by your assailant. Questions may still plague you: *Were you deep in thought as you walked to your car? Were you on the phone talking to a loved one or handling a business call? Were you too focused on getting to your car because of the weather, or maybe because you had to use the bathroom?* (*My grandmother, God rest her soul, called the latter "being in the tight."*)

Whatever the situation . . . it is not your fault!

Maybe you ask yourself if you complacently thought the daylight hours meant you were safe. Did you buy into the "you shouldn't have worn that outfit" lie? Are you thinking that you should not have parked next to the van at the supermarket? Are you kicking yourself for not seeing the signs? *What signs?!*

IT IS NOT YOUR FAULT!

You are not weak or weak-minded. It does not matter if you screamed or were paralyzed with fright. I do not care if you did leave your pepper spray on your dresser that day by mistake.

Let it go. Let it all go.

Your sexual trauma is not your fault!

You did not ask for it.

You did nothing but experience it.

We have to stop doing this to ourselves. Retrospection can lead us to doubt our inner strength, our self-preservation skills, and our love of self. Don't get me wrong; I get it. We are human, and as humans we try to analyze situations (both good and bad) so that we can do whatever we can either to prevent it from happening again or to make sure our success is repeated.

As stated earlier, retrospection can also be a good thing. We can choose what we want it to be. It can be a source of blame or a source of enlightenment. It can make us wonder whether we did everything in our power to prevent what happened or impel us to use everything in our power to press on toward our own form of healing. It can help us lose ourselves in the pain and feed our self-doubt or find and nourish our inner strength. Instead of a broken record playing the song titled "Woulda, Shoulda, Coulda," it can play a new song titled "Will, Shall, Can!" With a good support system that includes a certified therapist, YOU CAN.

Trust the process. Take your time on your journey toward your form of healing. The fastest runner does not always have endurance.

Dear Caregiver . . .

This is a lot to take in, I know. There are many pitfalls to avoid, many emotions with which to contend. You may not be able to handle hearing about a survivor's trauma. Own that. As a caregiver, you may worry about saying or doing the wrong thing. That is a good place to be. Stay there. It will cause you to think before you say or do anything. We appreciate that.

When a survivor approaches you for help, know that they may have already gone through this process of retrospection. Or perhaps they will begin that journey with you. It does not matter what stage they are in. It will not be easy. Not for you, but especially not for the survivor. Remind them that it is not their fault! They did not do anything to warrant what they experienced.

As the next chapter expounds, sounding the alarm is scary. Sometimes survivors immediately seek help. Other times we are so paralyzed with fear, disbelief, or denial that we refrain from telling anyone until we cannot take the pain residing within us anymore, and we need to release it. It is not your prerogative to share your opinion on that. No matter when a survivor chooses to tell their truth, it is the right time for them. I understand that for legal action to be taken, time is often of the essence, especially if evidence needs to be gathered. If a survivor did not follow this route, however, what good would it do to suggest that they should have, or to question why it took them so long to come forward? It does not matter! Just be there for them!

You may be the first person to whom a survivor tells their sexual trauma. In chapter 6, "Listen. Validate. FULL STOP," I assert that the first thing we want you to do is listen. Really listen. Do not think about how you will respond while they are speaking. Do not think about what could have prevented the sexual assault. We do not need or want you to analyze us or our trauma. We simply need you to listen. And then, once we are finished telling our truth, we need you to validate our stories. Tell us that you believe us.

If you too are a survivor of sexual trauma, this is not your time to share, and it definitely is not your time to compare stories. And never, ever, use the phrase "At least . . ." Once a survivor has finished sharing their truth, then perhaps you can inform them that you too are a survivor, only in the spirit of solidarity rooted in support and love. The underlying sentiment of you telling your truth is to say, "I am here for you."

Be careful, however, that you are not triggered yourself during the encounter. Being triggered means experiencing something that causes a negative emotional response. When encountering a fellow survivor, it may cause you to have flashbacks of your own sexual trauma and other sorts of painful emotions. Be fully aware of the impact on your own experience (see chap. 7).

Your own sexual trauma will undoubtedly inform how you will respond in your encounter with a fellow survivor who came to you for help. Know your limits. Additionally, please note that just because you are a survivor as well, it does not mean that you can say, "I understand." There is going to be something about their trauma that you did not experience. It is not a "cookie-cutter" experience.

We would rather you take a moment to take it all in before

you rush into reassurances and promises that will not be fulfilled. It is nice to say that a survivor will be okay, but do you really know that? How? What are you planning to do to make this happen? How do you know the survivor is open to what you have in mind?

If you must immediately respond, just say, "I am sorry. I am sorry that you experienced that." And take cues from the survivor for any next steps. Ask questions about how they would like you to proceed.

Just because a survivor "sounds the alarm," it does not mean that they are ready for immediate action or for their truth to become public, at least not at first—if at all. Each survivor is different, but this is something to consider.

Be gentle with us, and encourage us to be gentle with ourselves. Do not touch us! This is especially the case if there is a gender difference between the survivor and the caregiver. Always ask first if touching to provide comfort is acceptable, even if you intend the most gentle pat on the arm.

Be patient with us and encourage us to be patient with ourselves. Tell us that you will be here for us, even if it is to drive us to a counselor, a local sexual assault crisis center, legal authorities, or simply to get a cup of coffee to decompress after a therapy session. Just be supportive presence. We may just want you to sit silently with us. And at other times, we may want you to help us escape for a while by doing something fun or distracting us by telling us about your own life (especially if it is entertaining).

This chapter eases you into being a caregiver. Each chapter

will reveal a little more. As noted in the introduction, the directives in this book are solely based on my experience and thus are not exhaustive. I am describing just one way—*my way*—to respond when someone is sexually abused.

2

Find a Certified Therapist

Counseling helps. It may not heal, but it helps. In addition to other suggestions made in chapter 1, I want to emphasize the need for seeing a trained therapist.

I describe the years of counseling I had (and continue to have) as a wild roller-coaster ride. I am not talking about the modern-day ones with the best technology and fastest speed but rather the ones from back in the day, made solely of metal and wood that you heard squeaking and creaking at every turn. I held on for the ride, but every so often I would have to grab the safety bar, holding it tightly, and pray that I would make it to the end. When the ride was over, the rush overtook me. At times it turned my stomach. Other times it was invigorating. But without fail, I jumped on that ride again and again. Do you ride roller-coasters?

Therapy, my wild roller-coaster ride, has helped me significantly, but I have a long way to go. It has not healed me. It helps me to be gentle with myself on my journey toward my own form of healing. It gives me tools to help ward off the automatic feelings of self-doubt, self-blame, and self-critique that I impose on myself for not saving or protecting myself from my sexual trauma. My therapist walks with me during my tough bouts of retrospection. She is nonjudgmental and pastoral and calls "bullsh*t" when necessary. I need all aspects of her. I am blessed to have her.

She helped me to name what happened to me. "Say the words, Shanell. He . . ."

That was one of the most difficult things to do, because saying it aloud somehow made it more real. Although it already is real, having lived through it and talking about it feel like different experiences. Traumatic experience on repeat. Each time I tell my truth, I remember. And then, I had to remember myself, my well-being. This was especially the case when I told someone who did not believe me, or responded with an off-handed retort such as, "I am not choosing sides."

If you have not already done so, go to counseling or a sexual assault crisis center. Despite how awful it feels to reexperience your trauma, find someone. Although you may be embarrassed to retell what happened to you—as if the person can see you exposed—go and talk to a professional. Trust me, it helps. There is no fix-it pill we can swallow to erase the pain and memories. (I would have a stash.) Therapy is not a quick fix. I wish I could say that it is. It is a journey, a long, winding road, but if you have a therapist, you have a great traveling companion.

They can hold your hand when you get scared (if you can tolerate being touched). They can provide tissues when you cry. They will tolerate your use of bad words and sometimes use them themselves. They might even pray for you while you are there (and if you find a good one, when you are no longer in their presence). They will teach you how to take care of yourself and provide further resources if needed.

If you already have a therapist, perhaps you have experienced something similar. Maybe you learned ways to deal with the negative emotions you felt when you looked back on your sexual trauma and the events that led up to it. Perhaps they taught you how to deal with triggers. At any moment, something or someone can trigger your mind to go to an instant replay of what happened to you or some aspect of it. These can happen at the most inconvenient times, like at your female doctor's office when she has a male intern and asks if it is okay for him to perform an EKG. (This really happened.) Before my sexual trauma, I would be all for this. *Yes to furthering the education of future medical personnel!* After? Umm, no. Sorry, not sorry.

As a survivor, know that you have agency in situations like I had at the doctor's office. *All* health care professionals, not just therapists, should inquire about your level of comfortability. If they do not ask, advocate for yourself and say something.

Living post-trauma is markedly different than the life you lived prior to it. Hopefully your therapist helped you learn ways to deal with everyday life. If you are like me, you had to learn how to move past the hiccups you experience on a daily basis, such as someone simply touching you in a platonic way.

Having a therapist meant that I did not have to journey alone on the path of retrospection. It meant that when I felt bad for being an "easy mark," I had someone to snap me out of it, to help me make sense of it. I had new ways of understanding my experience, new ways of removing the blame from myself. But these new ways also resulted in more questions. I thought deeply over conversations I and my assailant had, picking them apart, searching for double or hidden meanings on which I did not pick up. It drove me crazy, but after each act of retrospection I had to remind myself:

It was not my fault!

A word of caution: I know it sucks having to retell your truth to new therapists. However, if you find that your therapist is not really listening to you—if they do not validate your truth, if they speak more about their experience guised as a form of solidarity, or they fail to provide any insight or ways of helping you cope—leave and do not return. Although therapy is hard, you should never feel worse than, or even the same as, the way you did when you entered their office, even if it is only 1 percent better.

3

It Is Never Too Late to Tell Your Truth!

"It happened a long time ago," he said.

Time. Time can function as a silencer. Too much time passing after our sexual trauma makes it harder to say something. "It happened a long time ago" is what a church leader said to my mother when she attempted to find some kind of recourse for what my assailant did to me. *So that's it? Nothing can be done? Nothing needs to be said to him?* This type of response is exactly why the chance of us telling our truth lessens over time. I know because this is what I felt.

Perhaps you heard something like, *"Why now? After all this time, what do you expect to happen? Did something recently happen to make you think of this? So much time has passed, and I've seen you interact with him. Certainly, you can see how troubling it is to hear this after all this time. My hands are tied. Why didn't you do or say anything before?"*

So what! So freakin' what! Time does not erase what happened. Time does not take away the assault. I am certain that no matter how much time has passed, you can still feel it! (*Ask me how I know.*) Time does nothing but age both you and your assailant.

But you can still sound the alarm!

You can still tell your truth! It is never too late. There is no expiration date. It may have happened a long time ago. But it does not lessen the truth of its occurrence. It does not decrease the amount of devastation we still feel.

Time does not erase trauma.

Do not let anyone put an expiration date on when you can sound the alarm. Voice your violent experience. Although there are statutes of limitations varying state by state in terms of seeking legal action, it does not prevent you from telling someone what happened to you.

Find a way to release it from within you.

Purge it!

4

"Sounding the Alarm" Is Scary

"What's the matter, baby? You haven't been yourself for a while now. Talk to me."

(I look into the tormented eyes of my wonderful husband, shake my head as tears well up in my eyes, threaten to fall over, and then grab my stomach and hunch over in the chair.)

(Now squatting down before me rubbing my back.) *"Baby, baby. Please. Please talk to me. Please."*

"Do you remember I told you that before we met something had happened to me—that someone had touched me inappropriately?"

(Deep breath.) *"Yeah. Yeah, I remember. That's what's been bothering you? It's in you, isn't it? You need to get that out of you."*

For the sake of the intimacy and privacy of my marriage, I have chosen to omit the majority of our conversation. This is how it ends:

After what could have been only a minute, but what felt like forever, I told him.

"It was ———! He touched me! Oh God!!!"

I do not know what my husband's facial expression was when I blurted out the name of the man who sexually assaulted me. I had fallen to the floor with my hands covering my head as I was overcome with body-wracking sobs. But I did not need to see his face. I did not need to wonder what he was thinking *about me*.

Because almost immediately, I felt his arms surround me. Comforting me through his own shock, anger, and pain. Holding me as I imagine his mind playing back of every single time that we were in my assailant's presence. Sitting at the table breaking bread together. Watching sporting events. My wonderful husband absorbed my cries and sobs with his strength as he kept a handle on his own. Clenching his fist as he recalled each time he shook the hand of my assailant. He had no idea. And yet, despite all of this, he said, *"I love you. I love you no matter what. I love you."*

And in that moment, the huge knot that dwelled within me got significantly smaller.

***

I was afraid to tell him. I was afraid he would not want me anymore. I was worried that he would look at me differently. With disgust. With contempt. Like he did not know who I was anymore. I was deeply concerned that he would consider me "dirty," much like I already thought of myself. Would he continue to show me affection? Would he think I was "used goods" because I was *used* for somebody else's screwed-up purposes? I did not want that. Not at all.

I was concerned that he would be upset with me because after all this time, I had never said anything to him. But I did not remember what had happened! I did not know if he would comprehend both what had happened *then* and that I had not remembered until *now*. I imagined him asking, *How did you not know? Why didn't you ever tell me who it was? I spent time in his presence! And you said nothing. You didn't warn me to stay away from him.*

I had played this conversation with my husband over and over in my head. Each time my imagination ended the conversation in failure. I was afraid he would think I was lying, or perhaps that I was making more out of something that was a simple misunderstanding. I was terrified that my husband would take matters into his own hands to avenge what was done to me. I was scared for what the possible responses would be.

I was incapable of thinking that he would do exactly what he did: love me anyhow. I did not think about the years of marriage we had together. I did not consider the love he has for me. I could not imagine that he would embrace me the way that he did. Fear had me in a chokehold, and I could no longer breathe or think clearly.

I thought my husband would not believe me when I told him that I did not remember what my assailant had done to me. That this was the reason I was able to function like "business as usual"—as if nothing was wrong, as if nothing had happened. This is why I was able to laugh at my assailant's jokes, sit at the same table as him during church functions, tell him he did a good job when he preached, and watch him get "filled with the Spirit" without myself being filled with disgust. I accepted invitations to social events he hosted. I even let him high-five my kids! He high-fived my kids! (*Lord help!*)

I did not remember what he did to me. I did not know that the hands he used to lay on me when I became an elder of the church would be the same hands that . . . I cannot even complete the sentence all these years later. I had no clue that when he helped serve communion and said the words of Jesus, "This is my body," that he could have been talking about mine. These are dangerous thoughts that proved not to be restorative or healthy for me to pursue. *Did he remember what he did to me?*

I did not. I did not remember until twenty years later. Twenty years is a long time, however, so when I told my husband what happened to me, it would only be about two-and-a-half weeks after I remembered my trauma myself. To me, it had *just* happened.

I could still feel his hands on me. After twenty years . . .

I should note that my fear of my husband's reaction was exacerbated by the fact that I had already "sounded the alarm" to someone else—a woman I thought I had a close relationship with—only a week prior. I did not receive a positive response from her. In fact, it was downright disrespectful, mean-spirited, and without compassion. My encounter with her intensified my fear of not being believed by my husband

and the possibility that his love was conditional, like hers. I speak about this in more detail in chapter 12, "There Is a Lot behind a S.M.I.L.E."

Looking back, I should have never let my interaction with this woman influence how I thought my conversation with my husband would go. I was so wrong about that. *Thank God!* Nevertheless, it does not negate the fact that the fear I felt before telling my husband was real. It was valid. It was troubling. It was crippling, paralyzing even. Perhaps this is why it took me over two weeks to tell him. Perhaps this is why once the memory of my trauma was released in my mind, I was overcome with incomprehensible apprehension.

I don't want to tell him. I can't tell him. I can't help but tell him.

Those three statements indicate the three different phases I went through prior to speaking with my husband. The first two phases occurred within a week's time after my memory returned. The third phase would begin during the second week and end unexpectedly the week after.

I don't want to tell him. This refers to how I felt the day the memory of my sexual trauma returned. I had just finished my text conversation with my assailant. I thought about the details of my sexual trauma. I thought about the deep betrayal of trust. I did not want to believe it had happened to me. *Nope. My husband does not need to know. We are doing really well right now. Everything is good. Our marriage is strong. Heck, I have gone this long without anyone knowing. I can do this. I can totally do this.*

I can't tell him. After a couple days of disbelief that I had that horrible experience, which morphed into immeasurable anger and shame, I began to feel guilty for not telling my husband. *You do not keep secrets from your husband, Shanell.* I knew this. This was a promise that we made to each other. However. *This is different. This. This could break us. He took something from me, but he cannot take my marriage. No. Absolutely not.* I was trying to justify why *not* telling my husband was an exception to our promise. Fear of losing him was beginning to take root because of all the "what ifs" running through my mind. I could not handle the thought of my husband being angry with me or getting arrested trying to defend my honor.

I was afraid of "sounding the alarm" to my husband. My husband! Someone that I love. Someone who knows me like the back of his hand. Someone who I know loves me wholeheartedly and unconditionally. Why was I still afraid?

Rejection.

I was afraid of being rejected by him. I was afraid of another prominent male figure in my life abandoning me. Cue in my little eight-year-old self. I was afraid that he would no longer be proud to call me his wife. I was afraid he would question the strength that I had within me. He calls me a strong black woman.

I was afraid because I could not lose him. Not him. I could not deal with the prospect of being abandoned by him. I could not tell him what happened to me because there was a lot at stake: my marriage, my children, and my husband's freedom, to name a few. I did not want to take the risk because I had a lot to lose. (I need to acknowledge that for some survivors, this loss is real. I need to remind you that this is *my* truth, and other survivors will have their own.) *I can't help but tell him.* Two weeks of remembering. Two weeks of self-doubt. Two weeks of anger. Two very long weeks of "what ifs." The incident, which, interestingly, I had not been able to call "sexual assault" at that time, had manifested itself as a huge knot in my stomach. It weighed me down. I felt it take root within me. In the pit of my stomach I felt pain, mental anguish, self-loathing, shame and embarrassment, fear of being rejected, fear of not being believed, frustration at myself for not being strong enough to have stopped it from happening, and dissatisfaction with my inability to move on from it *despite it.* All of this was tightly tethered together in the most achingly, panic-inducing, I-need-to-get-out-of-my-skin kind of way.

I could not eat. I could not sleep. My concentration was lost. Intimacy was a challenge. The knot grew and grew and grew. No matter what I tried—avoidance, escapism, pretending my sexual trauma did not happen—I could not get rid of it. I went to work with it. Cooked with it. Drove my kids to school with it. Took care of my family with it. I did everything with it festering within me.

I was trauma's helpless host, and it consumed me with its parasitic nature. It ate away all that I was, which I could no longer identify. *Did I ever know who I was, since I was always trying to be what I thought others wanted me to be . . . so they would not leave me?*

Why did my brain have to release this trauma back into my active memory? *Why didn't you stop this from happening, God?* Why could it not stay hidden far, far, far away in the recesses of my mind? Why could I not continue living without the knowledge of what he did to me? Why? Why? Why?! I was happy. *I think.*

And then, on that fateful day of July 10, 2015, I just couldn't take it anymore. I could not fake it anymore. My body would not contain it anymore. My body was purging it before it killed me. And it would have.

I *had* to let it go. I had no choice in the matter. My body went into protection mode *again.*

I *had* to utter those words. Keeping them inside was no longer an option.

My husband (then of twelve years) knew that *something* had happened to me before we met. He knew over the course of our marriage, from previous half-conversations and subtle hints, that someone had touched me inappropriately. In a way that made me uncomfortable with touch. In a way that made him realize he did not have 100 percent of my mind, body, and soul.

And he dealt with it.

On the day of the most difficult conversation I had with my husband, it ended with him telling me that he loved me. And on that day, my husband became my 100 percent. Thank God for my husband.

Sounding the alarm is scary.

Even to the people you love.

Especially them.

Dear Fellow Survivor . . .

I know it is scary. Trust me, I know.

Having gone through sexual trauma is bad enough. Having to talk about it seems worse, or at the very least, an extension of the trauma. Do people know that in order to "sound the alarm," it means that we must relive it? If the person we go to for support does not help us, we have to turn to someone else. If we decide to take legal action, we have to relive it then. For all the many times that we have to let others bear witness to what we went through . . . it is too much!

I hated writing this book even though I believe in it. I hate having first-hand knowledge of what sexual trauma is, and yet I hope my experience can help someone else. I hated having to relive what my assailant did to me. The constant writing, rewriting, and editing was too much to bear. I had to solicit prayers and texts of encouragement from friends to keep me from falling deep into an emotional, depressive state. I had to depend on several friends and colleagues to read chapters of my book and provide feedback because I just could not read it and relive it anymore. *Experiencing* trauma. *Talking* about the trauma. *Writing* about the trauma. I feel tertiarily traumatized. But it was worth it. I am worth it. You are worth it.

I know "sounding the alarm" hurts. It seems to elongate the pain. It stretches out the horrendous ordeal. Add to that the impending, unpredictable, and often inept responses of the hearers, and the emotional taxation goes to another level. It is tough to be open about what happened, right?

Opening our mouths to utter words that create a slow-motion picture in the minds of others is hard. It makes us feel extremely vulnerable. And if you are like me, you try your best to avoid feeling vulnerable because it makes you feel weak. It makes us feel defenseless *again*. And we have had enough of that.

"Sounding the alarm" is your choice!

I am not going to tell you that you must tell someone what happened to you. That seems to be pounded into our heads when we hear people and organizations talk about sexual violence survivors, and they prefer to call us victims. I intentionally do not refer to us that way.

I understand the imperative to tell someone. I can think of a few reasons. Perhaps they are concerned with the pursuit of justice. They may be concerned that a sexual violator is walking freely about, possibly lurking around for their next victim, setting the trap, laying the groundwork (*just like my assailant did to me*). In this case, we are told to tell someone *immediately* because the collection of evidence is time-sensitive.

Some of us will need to tell someone just so that someone else can be a witness to our truth. Perhaps the assailant is dead, and the survivor needs to purge it from within just to feel better themselves. In this case, "sounding the alarm" might not seem applicable because telling is not done to signify a warning or an alert that an action needs to be taken. However, I still think "sounding the alarm" is useful in these cases because there are times when a survivor "tells" their truth without knowing that they are "sounding the alarm." I find this to be the case especially for women of color, for whom justice is not expected to work. Women of color often are not trusting of and do not have confidence in systems of justice because those very same systems are the ones that created and maintained the stereotypical notion that women of color are lustful and hypersexual beings whose bodies are for the taking (#colonialmentality).

Sound the alarm!

I understand, however, that the guilt that comes with the imperative to tell is overwhelming. It is too much! Are we to add that to our already long laundry list of burdening emotions? What if we do tell, and nothing is done? What then? I am not providing reasons not to say something. I just need to make it clear that the imperative to tell comes at a cost. And we are the ones who usually end up paying it.

No one forced me to tell, but at the same time I did feel a certain amount of guilt when individuals asked me the identity of this person, and I did not divulge the information. One woman in particular became very upset with me (she still refuses to speak with me) because she says that there are other young girls in that church who may be in danger.

I get that. I do. I make no excuses. But I did what I was supposed to do. I did the best that I could. I gave the best that I had. Now I have to trust that the church leader with whom I shared my truth took the appropriate actions. I did not want to tell this person. At all. Nevertheless, I "girded my loins," made an appointment, and shared my truth *because* of those fatherless girls. *He works with the youth. He can't do that anymore.* I am unaware if anything was said or done to the man who sexually assaulted me. I have been "reassured," however, that several people in the church are aware of his identity, and they have taken "proper measures of protection" for the girls that remain. I remain skeptical.

Again, "sounding the alarm" is your choice. You may not be in the position or mindset to say something *right away.* Perhaps your mind and your body are no longer "in tune" with each other. Sounds weird, I know. But I felt disconnected to my body (after I remembered what happened to me). My body was not my own. It was not what I thought it was: clean and predator-free.

There was never an easy way for me to be in the right mindset for making decisions about "sounding the alarm." Even twenty years later, I could not reckon with it all. When I first considered doing it, I was overwhelmed with all the decisions I had to make. *Why couldn't this be easy?*

Do you feel the same way? Perhaps you are grappling with "sounding the alarm" as you read this book. You may be asking yourself, *Who do I tell? How much do I say? What parts do I keep private? How much is too much? Where do I have this conversation? What happens next? What if they do not believe me?*

If you are anything like me, you also have spent countless hours thinking about the various ways the scenario can play out. *If I say it this way, then . . . If I leave out this detail, then maybe . . . If I try to be strong and not cry, will my truth be less believable? If I do cry, will it seem that I am trying to be over the top? How much do I divulge? If I tell them what they did to me, will they see me naked? Will they go home and replay what happened to me in their mind for their own pleasure? Will they judge me? Will they gossip about me under the guise of procuring additional support for me? Will they do anything?*

These are all tough questions. They are real questions. Be gentle with yourself. And when you are ready to share your truth, my hope is that it goes well for you. That is the best advice that I can give. As I have already shared, I went through various stages of mental anguish and physical pain (the knot in my stomach) before *my body* took matters into its own hands. It was not until *after* I told my husband, and his positive affirmation of my truth and his unfailing support and love, that I was able to tell the other people who had the power to do something. This did not include the police because it was twenty years later. I thought it was too late to seek justice that way. So I told the people who had authority over him in a different capacity. Those who could stop him from doing what he did to me to another fatherless girl in the same setting. I told folks at the church. You will see how that turned out.

Although you may feel isolated and totally alone, know that there are many of us who have been where you are. Some of us decided to "sound the alarm," and others have chosen not to. You have to do what is best for you.

I am no expert. I only have my experience to offer you and

my analysis thereof. Telling my husband was the best decision I made, but I am only able to say this in retrospect. I did not know what the outcome would be. I did not have the same luck when I told certain other people. Those conversations did not go well at all. I told one person, and you know what I heard? Crickets. After I told her what happened to me, she said she was sorry that I experienced that, and then I heard nothing from her for weeks. Weeks! No call to check on me. No text messages. Radio silence. So I texted her to "check in." Do you know what she said to me? She told me that *she was not going to choose sides.* Imagine how that made me feel. A woman who happens to be "cool" both with me and the man who assaulted me said that she was not going to choose sides. But . . . that is exactly what she did. It hurt. It *still* hurts.

So, sounding the alarm will not be easy. You may not always get the results you desire, whatever that may be. But *go in knowing that.* They say that if we want to be disappointed, just set expectations. I *expected* her to choose me, to support me, and to be against him simply because she is a woman, and because I thought she and I were "close." I just *knew* she would choose me. There was not a doubt in my mind that she would be there for me. Boy, was I wrong. I am still not over it. To be rejected and cast aside, or to be on equal footing as the person who sexually assaulted you is not an easy pill to swallow. It hurts. Me versus him? And she was not going to choose sides? It hurts to delve into this any deeper. I just cannot do it.

If you decide to tell your truth, know that you may incur

both emotional healing and scarring. When I sounded the alarm, I found a depth of love, support, courage, and acceptance that I did not know was available to me. At the same time, I also experienced precisely the rejection that I most feared. Relationships changed or ceased to exist. You will never know unless you open your mouth and talk. I wish I had a surefire method to guarantee you the best results, but unfortunately I do not.

Unfortunately, there is also the case in which a survivor "sounds the alarm" not to seek assistance and care but to hurt someone else. When I contacted a close friend to follow up on our conversation in which I told her what happened, she lashed out at me. *"So what! Do you know that I was assaulted too? You are not the only person who was touched inappropriately. And yet the world is supposed to stop for you? For you?!"*

Yeah, that happened. In retrospect, I think she was projecting her own pain. Perhaps she was angry that I was able to seek help and/or justice for myself when she was unable to do so. Maybe she was silenced and ignored, and this was her opportunity to grab some of her stolen power back. Who knows? I am speculating here.

So I must ask, fellow survivor, what are your motives for telling? Was it an automatic response to hearing about someone else's trauma? Did this person who came to you make a case against someone that you are close to (which was what I did)? Perhaps you did not like the accusation. Perhaps you did not want your world to change just because someone else's did. It is possible that the assailant in someone's life might be the savior in yours. I make no judgments here.

How do we make sense of this? What if someone comes to us and shares their trauma without knowing that you are a survivor yourself? How will you react? We never know when the survivor will be asked to be the caregiver. That is not the role you need to assume. Do not feel pressured to be that for someone. Instead, refer them to someone who can.

I unknowingly asked a survivor to be my caregiver. I went to her for help not knowing about her experience. I am sorry to have heard about her own sexual trauma; however, I would have appreciated it if she told me that she could not fill that role. I cannot tell you how I would have responded if she told me this. I was a walking open wound. But I like to think that somehow we could have been there for each other.

Although our relationship was broken because of that encounter, if that close friend needed to hear my truth to compel her to release hers (despite the vindictive manner in which she did), then I guess I helped her to release it (at my expense). I wonder if she felt any relief.

I would not recommend "sounding the alarm" in a bitter, resentful fashion if it can be helped. I understand that we may be caught off guard by a survivor's truth. Hopefully, we can be supportive of each other. Solidarity can be a good thing.

"Sounding the alarm" is terrifying. But you can do it. I believe in you!

Dear Caregiver . . .

Have you ever been afraid of telling a horrible secret? Have you ever been at a crossroads where it is either you or the person you love? You had to choose to continue to suffer alone or to invite your loved one into the mess *with you.* Have you ever been afraid of losing someone because of something you went through that you could not control? How does fear manifest itself within you? Have you ever been so afraid to tell someone something because you thought it could end the relationship you had with that person? Have you ever kept something to yourself because you were afraid of how those you love would perceive you?

Welcome to our world.

A survivor thinks about how telling their truth will affect their relationship with the person in which they choose to confide, that is, if this person is not a professional counselor who is a stranger. They consider whether their relationship with the person will change or end. They wonder if their loved one will look at them differently and whether they will believe them or reject them. *Fear of rejection is real!*

Survivors contemplate whether their loved one will be upset or angry that they did not tell them sooner and whether they will doubt the veracity of their account. *What if they do not believe me? What will happen to our relationship? It will never be the same!* They think about whether their loved one will question their role in the assault. *What did you do? Why did they think that you wanted them in that way? Why didn't you stop it?*

The questions of uncertainty fueling the frightening experience abound. This is whether the caregiver is a loved one or a person in a position of authority from whom they seek assistance. When a survivor is considering "sounding the alarm," skepticism is tough to overcome. It takes loads of courage, strength to move past paralysis, and a certain amount of *umph* to utter the first word.

But we press on. We make the call and go to speak with the person we have chosen to help us because we do not have any other options. Often when survivors "sound the alarm," it is because We simply could not take it anymore!

"Sounding the alarm" is an exercise in vulnerability. As a survivor tells you about their sexual assault, they are exposing themselves. Each word they utter is like taking off a piece of clothing, and when the retelling is complete, not only are they naked, but they are exposed, stretched out wide—nothing is hidden.

Telling precedes viewing. As survivors, we know that sharing what happened to us paints a vivid picture. The more details are shared, the more the hearer is able to "see" what happened. And we know that you are seeing our assault with our bodies positioned and our faces strained and in pain.

We also know that if we omit the details of our assault, the hearer may think of any and all forms of assault about which they are aware, and the survivor plays a starring role in the remake. More important, they may think that the term *assault* does not apply because the details that were omitted are the ones that would "prove" the horror.

Telling is also difficult because it can also be viewed as exposing a weakness in the survivor. Because we could not handle it or cope on our own, we need to seek help. *What does that say about me? Why can I not handle this myself? Am I not strong enough? Why can I not move on?*

Telling is like a secondary assault because we are reminded about our initial defenselessness during the assault, and now we feel defenseless *yet again* having to ask for help. *Why am I not enough? Why can I not handle this on my own? What is wrong with me? I am a strong person, and yet ...*

Telling is therefore exhausting. It takes a lot out of us. Planning. Thinking. Weighing out the costs. The responses. After I told my husband what happened to me, the crying and violent shakes of my body left me spent. The build-up to the conversation drained me. Forming the words to retell my assault resulted in fatigue. I was weary and worn out. And I never felt more relief than that moment.

Although telling includes trust in the person sought out—whether a personal or professional support person—it also includes lots of concern and worry about whether we made the right decision. *Will this person really help me? Will my business be all over the church before I get home? Will they do something about this, or was my sharing my truth just a point of information? What will happen now? What do I do now?*

The moment we finish sharing about our sexual trauma is an important one. The ball is now in your court as the caregiver. What you do or say next is the decision maker. It determines whether we made the right decision in choosing you to help us. It lets us know whether you were the right person for sharing our most intimate, shaming, and horrific details about our sexual trauma.

One of two things may happen. We may find whatever is on the floor *very interesting* because we cannot bring ourselves to look you in your eyes. We may be extremely embarrassed, ashamed, or afraid to witness your reaction. Alternatively, *you* become the specimen under the microscope as we wait for you to respond, and all the while we are looking for any reaction on your part, both verbal and nonverbal. *Do they shift their position in the seat? Did they take a deep breath or make a snort? Do they look everywhere except at us? Are they fidgeting?*

If you do not know what to say, say that! *I do not know what to say.* We appreciate it if you stutter. It is an indication that we are not alone in viewing our trauma as incomprehensible. The trauma that we experienced is unfathomable! *Who could do such a thing?! You would be surprised!*

We need you to listen and be there. Prove yourself compassionate and understanding, even if you only function as a shoulder to cry on. If you find that you do not know how to help the survivor who has come to you for help, own it! Be upfront and transparent with us. If you do not do this, there is a chance that we will think you do not believe us and that you simply do not wish to help us. Say to us, "I don't know what to say. I was not prepared for this." And then, after asking the survivor if it is okay to do so, Refer, Refer, REFER! I will talk more about caregiver limitations later in the book.

What you need to know is that "sounding the alarm" takes energy and strength, both of which we as survivors may not have at the time. It takes energy and determination to not only conjure up the words that will recount and make the violence that we experienced real again, but even more courage to actually utter them.

It takes energy to hold close the door to all the "what ifs" and the "should've, would've, could'ves" that repeat in our minds as we tell our truth. Like footnotes in a book, they further support what is being said in the main text, but rarely do folks read them. But they are there. A caregiver must be willing to read these footnotes—to discuss the "background noise" that goes along with what is being verbally communicated. These thoughts constantly plague a survivor's mind, and thus it takes extra *umph* to say what we need to say.

Every conversation in which a survivor has to "sound the alarm" can either help or further harm them. The support I received from my husband helped to chip away at the heavy weight in my gut. He helped to ease the pain. He could not completely excise it, because there were more people with whom I needed to share my truth, and I was anxious about their response and reaction. Nevertheless, my husband took a huge chunk of that knot in my stomach away. He took away my concern that my relationship with him would cease or never be the same. Once I knew that I had nothing to worry about on that front, he was able to help me carry the rest of my burden by being there for me as I continued the scary yet pertinent task of "sounding the alarm."

As you will read, not all of my encounters with potential caregivers went as well. Often my truth was discounted, comfort was denied, and blame was placed on me. My burden was made heavier. Not only did their negative, harsh reaction replay the tape of my own self-doubt, but it also made me question my relationship with that person. *Had I misinterpreted how close we were? Were they deceiving me all these years? How could I not see this person for who they really are?* Again, we circle back to the question, *What is wrong with me?*

When someone who has been sexually abused approaches you for help and comfort, reflect on these things. Affirm their courage to "sound the alarm." Let them know that you cannot imagine how hard it is for them to come forward. *I admire your courage to tell your truth. It could not have been easy.*

Start there.

"Sounding the alarm" is trauma in and of itself.

Realize this. Understand this. Consider this when you are asked to help bear the load.

5

Fellow Survivors: Not Everyone Wants to Be Your Caregiver

I am sorry to be the bearer of bad news, but this is true.

Not everyone *wants* to be your caregiver.

They may not be able to handle your trauma and will "take a pass" on this responsibility.

That is okay.

Respect that.

Move on.

Not everyone wants to be *your* caregiver.

Not everyone to whom you "sound the alarm" will care.

Some will simply not believe you.

No matter what you say. No matter the "evidence" you have.

Some will tell you they believe you, but their actions suggest otherwise.

Some of these folks will be family members or close friends.

They may disappoint you.
You may question their loyalty.
They may show you their true colors.
It hurts.
It hurts really bad.
Feel what you feel.
But don't give up.
I know it's hard.
But PRESS ON.
You will find the caregiver you need.

6

Listen. Validate. FULL STOP.

I reached out to a church leader to tell her it was urgent that I speak with her. I did not tell her what I needed to speak with her about, but I told her it was urgent. I knew that there were other children and women at risk of the same thing happening to them. She set a date and a time, and I went to see her.

When I told her about my sexual trauma, I tried to do it in a detached, clinical fashion. This was not only because I was all cried out but also because the primary reason for this visit was not about me.

I told her, "He befriends young girls who are from broken homes where a father or father figure doesn't exist. Then he attempts to fill that void. He's friendly, caring, and has your best interests at heart. He's there for you if you need something. He's that uncle, that older male cousin with whom you can let down your guard. And then, when you reach the age of eighteen . . . he'll strike."

Yes, I wanted support for myself. I cannot lie about that. How-

ever, I also "sounded the alarm" to this person because I wanted to protect other young fatherless girls in the church from becoming a "survivor" themselves. This man is clever, well mannered, convincing, and always invested in the youth.

I was afraid for them, and I thought it was my duty to make the church leader aware of who was in their midst.

So I "sounded the alarm."

And when I was done, she said two sentences to me. The first I unpack in the next chapter. But the second thing she said to me, which I address here, was, "You're gonna be alright."

***

I was so glad that she did not interrupt me when I told her what happened to me. What a relief that was! I could not bear stopping and restarting. I am so glad I was able to get through it without her butting in.

Okay. I said what I came here to say. Now, I wait.

After a few long deep breaths she said, "You're gonna to be alright."

I'm gonna be alright? Alright?! When? How do you know? Are you going to help me become alright? What does alright even mean? Does it mean that I will be healed? In what way? Does it mean that I will forget what he did to me? Does it mean that I will remember what he did, but still be able to do what I need to do? A "functioning" survivor? Does it mean that she will help me? Will I be alright because he will get what he deserves? (Do I even know what type of justice or punishment would suffice?) What does "You're gonna be alright" mean?

I was not going to be alright. Not years after she told me that I was. I am *still* not alright. But I am getting better with therapy and a good support system.

My initial reaction to hearing "You're gonna be alright" was excitement. *Yes! Thank God! I am going to be alright! She is going to help me. She will do what she can to make sure that I am. I knew that she would not let me down. It was hard retelling my truth, but I am so glad that I did. I feel so relieved! Whew!*

My relief soon abated. (She made another off-putting, extremely horrific statement to me that I turn to in the following chapter.) My relief soon abated because that was it. I was told that I was going to be alright. Was it simply wishful thinking on her part?

I no longer felt relieved because there was no other form of comfort provided. I was hoping that she would support me in my time of need. I was hoping that she would *ask* me what I needed and/or wanted. I was hoping . . .

I was hoping that just maybe she would see through my calm, cool, collected disposition to see my pain, my shame, and my anger. I was hoping that since she knew me for many years, that it took a lot out of me to sit before her and share my personal trauma. Could she not see my hands shaking? Could she not see that I could not make eye contact? I kept my eyes anywhere but on her even after I had finished talking. Our eyes met only after I heard, "You're gonna be alright."

This was God's servant. God was speaking through her. This was God saying that God is with me, and that God will help me. That God will not let me down. (I speak more about how church leaders are often understood as being the mouth-piece of God in chap. 14.)

When she told me those words of assurance, I think I may have smiled a little. I thought to myself, *This is why I serve the God I serve.* God will help me through this church leader. God will make it all better, and she will be right there with me.

The room seemed a bit brighter. The air was easier to breathe. I felt a little more comfortable in my skin. Life will become a little bit more manageable. *I can do this!*

Yes, I would do this. Life would become a little bit more manageable, but it would not be because of this church leader. It would be because of others who have said, "I am here for you" and were actually there for me.

She said I was going to be alright, but those were just words. Empty words. Meaningless words. Words spoken just to have something to say. And maybe that was all she knew to say, but they proved meaningless because nothing else happened.

Nothing.

I kind of wished she had interrupted me to ask for further information, to get clarity on the when, where, what, and how. Ask me anything! Show interest! Show that I matter! Ugh!

While I believe her response came from a place of good intention, it fell flat because there was no further conversation to determine how she could help me. I was not comforted. She did not say that she would stand by me. She did not say, "I'm sorry you went through this." She did not say that measures would be taken to protect the other youth for whom I am concerned. She did not *ask*. She did not *do*. She did nothing.

Even more disheartening is that she did not validate my truth. She never said she believed me. She did not even try to disprove what I said. Not that I wanted her to. She did not ask if I had any proof (although it was twenty-plus years ago). She did not ask me anything! She did not make any comment about my truth. This only made me wonder, *Did she hear a word that I said? Does she believe me?*

I needed to hear that she believed I was telling the truth. Or at the very least, allow me to prove that I was.

Before I left her office, the room and my world dimmed. My skin felt tighter. It did not fit. I wanted out of it. The air got thicker. I could not breathe easy. I left there feeling worse than when I went in. I left there disappointed with her lack of ministerial care. Of me!

I am a daughter of the church! I did so much for this church. I ushered. I sang in the choir. I taught Sunday school. I was an elder. I ran Vacation Bible School. I preached the Word of God from the pulpit! I accepted the call to ministry here! I got ordained here!

Does none of this matter? Does nothing need to happen because I no longer attended the church? Is it because I moved, and so nothing (at least for me) needed to be done? What about me? Do I not matter anymore?

I thought . . . I thought that if I did everything that was asked of me, then God . . . God would be there for me. God would use God's people to help me the way I help others. God would "show up" and do something through God's chosen leaders. What am I missing here, God? Did I do something? Why?

After I left her office, I would never return. There were no follow-up calls to see how I was doing. I got no updates about how my assailant's presence around or with the youth was altered or stopped. No measures were taken to reprimand him (that I know of). I seriously doubt it, because this church leader who assaulted me continued to read Scripture and preach from the pulpit.

Nothing changed. Nothing changed!

I thought that "sounding the alarm," speaking my truth, would create a storm that would cause a ripple effect in the church administration, but it didn't happen.

Thank you. Thanks for telling me. Have a good evening.

Nothing changed except my faith in God and God's people.

Oh! And me. I changed.

When I left her office, not only would I leave my respect and (most of) my love for that church leader, but I also left (most of) my love for God and the church.

If this is the God she says I should serve, then no. No thank you.

Dear Fellow Survivor . . .

You did it.

You went to someone and "sounded the alarm." You mustered up all of your energy, *temporarily* cast away your fears regarding telling, and persevered despite any consequences that may come about because of it. You put yourself first and let it all out to someone you thought would help care for you.

Maybe, like me, you have a great sense of gratitude because you got to tell your story without being interrupted.

As I mentioned earlier, I do not know if she made any facial expressions because I did not want to make eye contact as I spoke about my painful experience. I also did not hear any murmurs or grunts. I only heard the sound of my voice uttering the most horrid of things that happened to me.

She did not stop me. She did not cause me to pause. She did not interrupt me and cause me to begin a part of my truth from the beginning.

I was grateful.

If you are anything like me, I wanted to get my trauma out of my mouth with the utmost haste. Like ripping off a bandage, I thought if I spoke fast, it would be over quickly and cause the least amount of pain.

I also know that if she interrupted me, it would have irritated me. It would have lengthened the time it took to tell my truth. It would have eventually led to me leaving out pertinent details or chunks of my truth just to get it over with.

Depending on the types of questions that were asked, including questions that made me feel defensive or threatened, I might have stopped talking altogether and walked out.

Perhaps you feel similarly. How was it when you told

that first person? The second? The third? Did it get easier with each time? Or does that depend on who your audience is? Did you tailor the story differently—omitting certain details—depending on whom you were speaking with? Did you have different expectations for the people to whom you told your truth?

When you spoke, did they interrupt you? How did it make you feel? Maybe this is not as much of an issue for you as it was for me. And that is totally fine. This book expresses *my* experience, which is not everyone's. There are no cookie-cutter experiences. Hopefully you felt that they at least listened to what you shared.

Then what happened? Did you get the assistance you needed? Did they attempt to console you? Did they cry with you? Did they ask if you have spoken with the police or any other kind of authority? Did they ask if you were okay?

Did they touch you? How did that make you feel? Was it a source of comfort, or did it make your skin crawl? Did you inch away when they came to sit next to you? What is a safe distance for you?

Before you met with them, had you considered how the conversation would go? Did you know how much you would tell? Did you wonder if they would believe you? Did you have an idea of what you needed from them? Did you know what you wanted to happen?

What does justice look like for you? What did you want to happen to your assailant, especially if they attended the same church as you? What did you expect would happen when you told your church leader? Do you want to have a "sit down" with the person who assaulted you? Although it was not an option presented to me, I do not know if that was something I would have been open to doing.

I wish I knew then what I know now (and I am still learning). I wish I knew how to probe her for answers. I wish I knew how to take control of the situation. I wish I knew how to push back against the insufficient response I received, and the resulting silence and inaction. I wish I knew how to be my best advocate. I wish.

I hope that your experience went better than mine did. I hope you received both emotional and physical support (if needed). I hope your load was lightened because the person from whom you sought help has decided to help you carry it. Consider yourself blessed if you had or have that. I am very happy for you.

If you have not yet "sounded the alarm," please be sure to read the previous chapter.

If you have, I commend you for saying something in the first place. As we discussed in the last chapter, "sounding the alarm" is scary. It is not easy. Regardless of the outcome, you should feel good about yourself for taking that step.

If you have chosen not to "sound the alarm," I support you as well. Whatever your reasons are, I believe that your decision is what is best for you. And if you do not feel safe telling someone your truth, I hope that that changes for you, and that not only you *feel* protected but that you *are* protected.

Thinking about my encounter with a church leader, I realize that I was not as prepared for it as I thought I was. I thought I could just show up, blurt out what happened to me, and then let my listener take over. I thought that she would know what to do. I thought that all the responsibility now resided with the church leader. She would take care of me. I had "sounded the alarm." Now she had to deal with it.

I think differently now.

On the one hand, I believe that a church leader *should* know what to do. I understand that they might be taken aback by our trauma. *Take a minute to regroup!* They should be aware of any sexual harassment and assault policies for their church (if they have one), and they should offer to go with you if you need to go to the police or a sexual assault crisis center (see chap. 15).

On the other hand, I should have been more prepared. I knew what parts of my truth I would keep to myself (some details were unnecessary to tell) and which ones I would divulge. Although that was the hardest part to say, it was the easiest part to figure out.

What I did not do *beforehand* was think about what I wanted to happen. I should have asked myself the same questions I posed to you. Hopefully this book will help you before you have that conversation. Hopefully you'll never have cause to have that conversation.

As a survivor who may have shared their truth, you know the importance of being heard and of having one's truth validated. You know that getting your truth out uninterrupted helps us get through it—not only in terms of time but also in terms of revisiting our trauma.

There may come a time, however, when you as the survivor will be asked to function in the role of the caregiver. What will you do? How will you respond? Will you be able to engage? Will you make comparisons? Will you be able to be there for that person? There is much to consider here. The next chapter talks about how to respond when your own experience with sexual trauma interferes with or impacts your encounter with a fellow survivor.

Dear Caregiver . . .

Listen. Validate. FULL STOP.

Sounds simple enough, right?

It may not be as simple as it sounds.

What will your reaction be when someone "sounds the alarm" to you? Often when a survivor tells their truth, it will be without warning. When they ask to meet with you, more often than not they will not say, "I need to meet with you to tell you that I have been sexually assaulted." No. It does not happen that way.

A survivor only wants to tell you about their trauma once. They do not want to give you a preview of their trauma. They will not say to you, "Get ready, because I have to tell you something really, really bad."

Well, to be quite candid here, I did say something to this effect to someone before I met with her. I said to her, "When I tell you this, relationships will be changed." I was wrong about that. You see, I expected her to choose me. I expected her to state her allegiance. To me. She did not. I realized that my comment to her was overly confident not only because of what I thought her response to me would be but also because I thought that she would do or say something to my assailant on my behalf. *Because* of me. I was wrong. But I digress.

A survivor will *most likely* not give you a preview of what they want to share with you. You will most likely be caught off guard with what they have to tell you. What will you say? How will you respond? What will you do? (I talk more about this in chap. 15.) For now, the first thing you need to do is Listen.

This may be the hardest part for you. Listening to the trauma of a survivor. They may give you every detail, zoning out as if they are reliving it. They may just give you blocks of information: who did it, where, and when.

Listen.

What you hear may make your skin crawl. It may change your perception of the assailant (if you know them). It may change your perception of the survivor. In what way? I do not know. However, you may never look at either the assailant or the survivor in the same way again. Hopefully you will see the survivor as a person of strength and perseverance.

Listen, and keep listening. Pregnant pauses may happen. Wait. There may be moments of crying. Wait. A survivor may need to regroup. Wait.

Look for the cues. They may look at you once they are done talking. They may use words to indicate the recounting is finished. If you are unsure, ask them if they are done. But please be gentle with your tone. Tone is important.

After you are certain that they are finished stating their truth, validate.

You can begin by saying, "I am sorry that you experienced that" (or something to that effect).

By saying that you are sorry *that they experienced that*, you are confirming not only that you heard what they had to say but also that you believe that they went through the ordeal they described.

As a church leader or someone with power to make a decision concerning justice or some means of recourse, validation may be tricky. You may want to withhold validating a survivor's truth until you hear the other person's perspective (if you know them). Do not do this. Validate the survivor's truth immediately.

Someone might argue that validation should wait until both parties have been questioned, because to "validate" means to confirm that something is true.

Yes, that is a definition. However, when it comes to a survivor of sexual violence, validation must come immediately because their account is their truth. Let me repeat: A survivor's account is their truth.

It is what happened to them. Believe them.

It may sound trivial, but try to be intentional about using the word *truth* instead of *story*. The word *story* can also mean a lie, a tale, gossip, or hearsay. If the survivor had a similar upbringing like mine, the primary definition of the word *story*, in this context, meant a lie. Growing up, we were not allowed to say someone "lied" but rather that they told a "story." To refer to a survivor's account as a "story," therefore, might initially throw them off. They might think that you do not believe them.

Perhaps if one explicitly says, "I believe your story," this misunderstanding can be avoided. However, if one were to say, "I heard your story," that can suggest that you heard the lie they told. It may not be an issue for many survivors, but it is for some. Like it is for me.

For this reason, I intentionally employ the word *truth* throughout this book. It is hard enough to open our mouths. There is no need for a survivor to be offended or taken aback by word usage when it can be avoided.

Hear a survivor's truth, and believe it immediately.

Listen. Validate. Full stop.

Now what? What should your next steps be?

Whatever they are, they should be made *in consultation with* the survivor. You need to determine what the survivor wants to do, if anything. If you are a caregiver in a position of power, you may be a mandated reporter. Do you know what that means? It means that due to your profession, you may be legally required to report the assault to the authorities. I do not know if your church polity has its own rules and protocols that you need to follow. You need to find this out. Be familiar with and consider the laws and stipulations pertaining to this situation.

As a church leader, you may have different questions. *If I validate the truth of the survivor, does this mean I do not need to listen to the "truth" of the person they said sexually assaulted them? I am a church leader to both parties, so how can I choose sides when I am supposed to care for both of them? Do I help the survivor but not the assailant? What about forgiveness?*

These are all real questions a caregiver may need to consider, which is why I dedicate an entire chapter to it (chap. 15). Before we get there, however, let us reconsider the encounter between the survivor and the caregiver, but this time, as a caregiver who is *also* a survivor.

7

When the Caregiver Is Also a Survivor: The Impact of Your Own Experience with Sexual Violence on the Encounter

I reached out to a church leader to tell her it was urgent that I speak with her. She set a date and a time, and I went.

I told her, "He befriends young girls who are from a broken home where a father or father figure isn't present . . . And then, when they reach the age of eighteen . . . he'll strike."

I was afraid for them, so I "sounded the alarm."

I told her everything. *What I could remember from start to finish.*

She shook her head left to right. Paused. Took a deep breath, and then without making eye contact, she said, "I'm just glad you weren't raped."

Then, after another long pause she said, "You're gonna be alright."

***

I told her what he did to me. From beginning to—well, I cannot say "to the end" because as I have said earlier, I do not remember all of what happened to me. One moment I am describing what he is doing to me, and the next thing I remember is being home. It is like I blacked out.

I told her in stark detail everything that I remembered, hoping that each element of my retelling would make her believe me.

I needed her to believe me.

I needed her to say that she would handle it. Fix it. Do something. *Anything!*

I needed her to ask me what I needed.

I needed to know if she planned to put measures in place to limit his access to those girls.

I needed to know that my telling would result in something happening *to* him before he came *for* them. My telling *had* to bring about some form of justice, protection. It just had to!

Because if it didn't . . .

If it didn't . . .

It. Didn't.

Because *she* didn't.

She didn't do any of the aforementioned, except maybe the

touched

first. I assume this to be the case because of my assailant's continued active presence in the lives of the youth as well as his preaching from the pulpit.

I think she believed me, although she never confirmed this. However, a careful look at and dissection of our conversation suggests that she may know all too well that the likelihood of what I said happened to me was very real.

Here is why.

While I recounted what happened to me, she did not move. She did not reach for me or try to hold my hand. She stayed frozen on the opposite couch where she was.

I do not know if she was holding her breath, but based on her body language, something rendered her motionless, immobile, emotionless. I assume that she was picturing what I described to her. I presume that perhaps she was shocked, like I disoriented her with a front-row view of my sexual assault. Was it too much? I know it was for me. Could she not imagine him—a respected church leader in the community—doing those things to me?

Or perhaps her silence and stoic posture was all she could do because as I described my sexual assault, it brought her own lived experience of sexual violence back to the forefront of her mind. (*I am leaning toward this possibility.*)

"I'm just glad you weren't raped."

Wow. To this day, her statement troubles me. However, I have learned that sometimes the worst, most off-handed, dismissive comments (whether or not the speaker's intentions are good) often emerge from a place of pain.

Although I have no proof that she had such sexual trauma—and I seriously hope she has not—the very first thing she said to me makes me at least consider that a possibility.

Perhaps she remained silent, never telling a soul of her trauma for reasons only she would know. And perhaps I just peeled off the scab of her own supposedly healed and scarred-over wounds, and the only thing she could muster up was a comparison.

"I'm just glad you weren't raped."

At first I was taken aback. When I got home, I got angry.

What does that even mean?!

You cannot quantify sexual assault with body parts!

At the time of our encounter, I did not know all of what had happened to me. I still don't. At one point during the retelling of my truth, I stopped and said, "And the next thing I know, I was home."

Recently, I spoke to my therapist about whether there was a possibility that I was, in fact, raped. Not to prove or justify any reason to say #MeToo (*I still have cause*) but because at that particular moment, I wanted to know. She told me that she thinks if that had happened, I would have remembered. I then asked her, "What if I was roofied?" Could that explain my lack of knowledge of what else happened to me? She says that I would have *felt* something the next day. I am not fully convinced of this. To be clear, I am not hoping or wishing that I were raped. I cringe to think of whether or not my assailant was "gentle" and eerily chuckle when I think that perhaps he is just "small."

I keep wondering if he had given me a date-rape drug. I have no idea. I would have accepted and drank a beverage from him that was already opened without question. He already had my trust. Does a person's memory return if they are roofied? How much do they remember? I have reached the edge of my ignorance here. Nevertheless, either he put something in my drink, or my brain still has not released the rest of my trauma because it is protecting me.

There is such a thing as temporary amnesia. Some call it a "window of amnesia." Simply put, our brains function as our protectors by putting the traumatic events we have endured "under lock and key." Perhaps we try so hard to forget what happened to us that eventually our minds lock away the memories for us, in a manner of speaking. Over time, it is as if the trauma never happened. Our minds compartmentalize. Our bodies go into survival mode, helping us to cope until it feels we are ready for those memories to be released. It may be when we have a good support system or a good therapist, or in my case, after we have moved a good distance away from where the sexual trauma occurred.

I still do not know *everything*. My mind is still protecting me until I am ready. I am not sure I ever want to be ready. Some days—when I am most courageous—I want to know. However, a majority of the time, I do not. I have nothing to prove to anyone. And yet I already expect that there will be someone who will downgrade my experience as *she* did because I cannot recall it.

Most of the time I hope that whatever else happened to

me is never released. It is hard enough dealing with what I already know. Even as I write this book, my prayer has been that my "window of amnesia" stays closed. I cannot handle more. I do not want to. I have enough fodder for this book.

When the church leader said, "I'm just glad you weren't raped," initially I was relieved. Whew! You're right. I was not raped. What I mentioned above about not remembering did not occur until I was in therapy. While talking about my encounter with the church leader with my therapist, I realized that her comment later caused further traumatization, hurt, and anger.

Somehow, she had placed my sexualized trauma on some sort of sexual assault scale, and my experience did not measure up.

There is not a hierarchy of acts of sexual violence.

She relegated my sexualized trauma to a position below those who have been—*who remembered that they were*—penetrated, raped. What I had experienced was not enough to count in her eyes. Not enough to warrant action of any kind on her part. No support was needed. No further conversation with me and/or the person who assaulted me should ensue. No follow-up to see how I was doing was necessary.

"Oh! He just touched you? I'm just glad you weren't raped. You're gonna be alright."

There is no such thing as "just" anything. I cannot recall if I was raped. I was not "gonna be alright" for a long while . . . and I am not yet there.

She was someone I trusted. Someone I loved. Someone I

had no doubts would be there for me and help me—even if we had to figure out what that was together. But she was not. Or perhaps, as I mentioned earlier, she could not.

She may have been triggered by my truth. When I described the location where my trauma occurred, she may have found herself back in her own. She may have recalled the color of the wallpaper, the dampness of a basement, the dust at the bottom of a cubicle, the stained-glass artwork of Jesus that hung on the wall . . . I could go on.

The point is, she may have remembered, and because of my "sounding the alarm" to her, she will have to work on remembering her body, mind, and soul. Triggering can happen anywhere and at any time, and this process of putting herself back together may be the hundredth time she had to do it. Or it could be the first time.

Had I somehow unlocked some things in her brain by sharing with her my own sexual trauma? Am I somehow at fault here? (*There goes that self-blame again.*) How was I supposed to know what she went through? Am I to feel bad about this? Should she have stopped me once she knew what I was about to say because she could not handle the details? Was she able to?

Thinking about all of these possibilities greatly lessens the amount of hate and severe disappointment that I felt for her. I feel bad for her. Certainly, her being a survivor herself is pure speculation on my part, but what if . . .

Just what if she is a survivor asked to be a caregiver?

Now what?

Dear Fellow Survivor . . .

We will not always know.

The person we choose to "sound the alarm" to may not be able to provide the kind of care, support, and/or justice we need. On the one hand, we may feel betrayed, disappointed, and angry that they did not do anything to help us. They did not say anything to comfort us. They did nothing! On the other hand, were they able to? Were they rendered paralyzed by our own trauma? Was their own pain triggered by ours? We will not know unless they tell us.

When the caregiver is also a survivor, the encounter can get complicated. Your pain clashes with theirs. The details of your truth become muted, and theirs become amplified. Like a deck of cards, the events of your sexualized trauma are mixed together, and everything is jumbled. However, neither party is aware.

As a survivor, you wait to hear what the caregiver will say in response to your telling. You begin to get uncomfortable with the silence (if there is one). You may be affronted by any quick retorts or empty phrases of comfort that result in no follow-through. You may rethink your relationship with this person (if you knew them), and it may never be the same.

The survivor-turned-caregiver may be lost for a few minutes. Their mind may need a minute or two to jumpstart. You may be waiting for them to respond to your trauma; however, they need a minute or two to control their reaction to their own. They may need time to compartmentalize. (*Get back in the box.*) Or we may have rendered them speechless because unbeknownst to us, our trauma functioned as the key to unlock the trauma locked away in their own mind.

But if the caregiver does not tell you this . . . if the caregiver does not know how to handle this . . . if the caregiver is unable to assist you . . . then what?

Communication is key! As evidenced by my situation described above, this lack of communication resulted in a major clash that strained and later ended a beautiful, flourishing relationship. I thought she was being dismissive and belittling of my trauma. And she was giving me the best she had. Perhaps that was all she had to give because she was triggered by what I said to her. Who knows? To this day, she does not know what her comments and lack of support did to me. (*Perhaps one day I will reach out to her.*)

Perhaps you have experienced something similar. It is possible that the caregiver you chose is also a survivor who has not dealt with their own trauma or still experiences flashbacks, PTSD, or the like if they are triggered. It could also be that your person has fallen prey to all the misinformation about sexual trauma that is out there.

Did they make you wonder if what you went through *was that bad?* Did you second-guess yourself? Did you wonder if you were making a big deal out of nothing? Did they make you feel like you had it easy?

The various ways that our sexual trauma can be relegated, diminished to *just* some form of touch, are plenty. I heard, "I'm just glad you weren't raped." You may have heard a response that began with the phrase, "At least." To begin a response with "at least" is not something we want to hear from a caregiver, right?

Whether or not the caregiver is a survivor themselves, it would not be in good form to say something with the words, "At least . . ." We do not want our experiences compared. It does not make us feel better. We are not interested in playing the game "Who Had It Worse?" There is no such thing! At no time do the words "at least" follow with something that makes us feel better about ourselves or what happened to us!

At least you didn't die. At least someone saved you before your assailant was able to do more. At least they were able to get samples. At least . . .

Please. Comparisons are not welcome.

I am all for people who say "Me too" in order to show solidarity in survival despite differences in race, sex, gender, age, and so on. I support those who say "Me too" in order to let a fellow survivor know that they are not alone and that they have someone who will hold their hand and be a good listener despite their own suffering. It is wrong, however, to say "Me too" in order to compare, contrast, compete with, and cast aside another survivor's truth.

Although it may not be the intent of the "me too" person, this juxtaposed, frame-by-frame examination of trauma can feel like a competition: who suffered more? This one-upmanship, intentional or not, is hurtful. To hear phrases such as "I'm just glad you weren't raped" and "At least . . ." silences us. It makes our stories seem inferior, not enough. It may even prevent us from telling anyone else. We begin to doubt the severity of what happened to us. We begin to question whether or not we are making a big deal out of something that *wasn't that bad compared to* . . . Stop. Just stop!

Give us permission to feel what we feel.

Do not compare your trauma to someone else's, and do not let someone else do it to you. A hierarchy of sexual trauma does not exist, and if it does (meaning someone created one), do not believe it! We only hurt ourselves in the process.

When we go to someone to "sound the alarm," we may not know if we are speaking with a fellow survivor. Hopefully, if you are reading this book prior to seeking help, my experience can help you. However, it does not always happen this way. You may find your caregiver lacking for different reasons. They may say the wrong thing—if anything. They may say all the right things—whatever is right for you—and then fail to check on you or follow through with any next steps the two of you may have determined.

No matter what, I encourage you to keep seeking the help you need. I "sounded the alarm" to several people. The first person said they believed me, then ignored me, and then discounted my truth. The second person believed me and offered full support but was not in a position of authority to reprimand my assailant and remove him from ecclesial office. The third person had no emotional response to what I said, gave two very short responses (one of which led to self-doubt about the severity of my assault), and then an empty promise since there was no follow-through. I kept reaching out. I kept "sounding the alarm." Why? I wanted to believe that there was someone out there who would do something. I wanted proof that the people who I believed loved me and would be there for me, would actually *be there for me.* Telling became a measure of loyalty based on the responses I received. Certainly, this is a faulty process. (Who else might be a survivor who has no idea of the effects of their trauma on my own?)

Nevertheless, I eventually found a few good folk who have been with me throughout this process of healing. It is a journey. A very long one. I do not yet see the end in sight. (Is there one?) But I do not have to journey alone.

I wish the same for you.

Dear Caregiver . . .

Are you a survivor?

Have you spoken to someone about it? Did you receive the help you needed? Are you in a position to help a fellow survivor? Are you easily triggered? Are you mentally in a position to be a source of support for someone else?

If you have not experienced *sexual* trauma, it does not preclude you from making bad comments, empty words of praise and promise, or comparisons with other forms of trauma you have experienced or what you may have read or heard from someone else.

The point of this chapter is to know yourself. Be aware of your experiences (sexual trauma or not) that will impact your encounter with a survivor. How well do you deal with conflict? Do you avoid it? Deal with it head-on? What will you do if the survivor does not want you to do anything, but just listen? Will you be able to honor their request?

I understand that it can get confusing. A survivor may not want you to do anything. A survivor may want you to take action. Part of your job as a caregiver is to take cues and instructions on actions from the survivor. If you are a survivor yourself, it does not mean that what worked for you will work for the one seeking care from you. Do not force anything upon them.

Often responses are made with good intention to help the survivor and make them feel better. And initially they may have a positive impact. *"You are gonna be alright."* Yes, yes I am! *How do you know? This person is going to help me be alright!*

First, do not say these things if you have no intention of making this happen or lack the means to do so. Second, how do you know? How do you know this survivor is going to be alright? Wishful thinking is good, but if it does not happen, *especially* for a survivor, then what?

Whether or not you are a fellow survivor, your encounter with a survivor who has decided that you would be the person to whom they "sound the alarm" will more often than not be unexpected. You will not see it coming. It will catch you off guard. And it will not be fun for either party. It will hurt the survivor to tell it. It will hurt you to hear it (at least it should). How will you deal with it?

If you begin with the phrase "at least," you may think that you are helping the survivor feel better about their trauma. *There is something worse that you could have experienced.* Suggesting something like this just does not help. While your intentions may be good, the self-doubt that results is not. Hearing such phrases makes the survivor feel belittled. It makes us feel like what we went through does not warrant further action or the emotion that we may presently exhibit. It makes us feel that our sexual assault is *inferior*, and that is a horrible feeling! Inferior to what? Someone who *really* experienced sexual trauma because they were raped? Sodomized? Cut with a knife as well?

There is not a hierarchy of acts of sexual violence. Since when did rape become the ultimate offense? Since when did one have to be penetrated—whether with a penis or some other object—in order to have one's traumatic experience validated? Likewise, there is no hierarchy of suffering in the wake of sexual violence.

Comparisons of either experience or suffering is not helpful, especially when used as a way to weigh gradations of suffering and/or violence. Since when did any one person's suffering trump someone else's? Suffering is relative to the person who experiences it. What constitutes suffering to me may not be considered suffering to someone else. How I react to and deal with suffering may differ as well. And that is quite alright!

Be careful of the things you say. They do not die once the encounter is over. They live on and influence how we as survivors engage others in dialogue about sexual trauma. What you say matters.

There is no hierarchy in terms of sexual assault (no matter

what you have heard or read). A survivor's experience is just that—*theirs*. It does not compare to any other survivor's experience, including your own. A survivor is not interested in sizing up pain and trauma.

A survivor chose you for a reason. Perhaps they know and trust you. Perhaps you are law enforcement or a therapist. Why they chose you does not matter. It is the encounter that matters. It is what happens and what is said in the encounter, and what you do and do not do following it.

Do not interrupt a survivor's retelling of their trauma unless you cannot handle it, or it triggers your own trauma.

Listen and validate what they tell you.

And for God's sake, do not make comparisons.

If you are a survivor and have not spoken with someone but need to, please find a therapist. Do this for yourself. You deserve it. The fellow survivor who will come to you for support will benefit from it.

You may be a survivor's first encounter. It makes an impression. Hopefully it will be a good one. If not, hopefully the survivor will still be encouraged to seek help elsewhere.

If you remember nothing else, remember to Listen. Validate. Do not interrupt.

As a caregiver—even if you are also a survivor—please be silent, and let the survivor speak. This is their time. Not yours. Be patient with them. Focus on what they are saying. Try your best not to compare your experience with theirs.

Do not interrupt a survivor when they are telling you about their trauma unless they say you can do so. They may tell you, "Just let me get through this," if you have not established the rules of the conversation. Do not be offended. This is tough for them.

Follow the survivor's lead. If they sit at a distance from you, go with it. Do not question it. They may not want to give clarifying information. What you get may be all you get. We may not have more to tell, or we have chosen not to divulge everything. Some details may be too hard to discuss. Stating them makes them that more real.

Be silent. Wait until they are done. You will get your opportunity to ask questions or share about your own trauma if they want to hear it.

However, if you find yourself being triggered by their truth, stop them.

As a survivor, you must protect yourself as well. Be gentle with them. Tell them that you are sorry that they have experienced this horrific trauma; however, you are unable to handle hearing any more. If you do not want to share your truth with them, say something like, "It hits too close to home." Then, if you are able, refer them to someone who can help them. Share any resources you may have.

I remember telling a colleague about what happened to me. As soon as I got through the first few lines, she began to share about her own experience. That would have been fine if she waited until I was done, and if she was not trying to make a comparison. However, she went "tit for tat" with me. I named a location. She named a location. And her assault happened in the daylight, as if that made hers worse. I said I knew my assailant. She said she was related to hers. I said I did not remember all of what happened to me. (See chap. 12.) She said, *"Oh! So you weren't . . . You didn't . . . I had . . ."*

As if we were playing a horrible game of sexual assault one-upmanship, she was determined to be the winner. *This is not a game that I wanted to win. I did not even want to play.* (To this day, I do not know why I let our conversation go on for as long as it did.)

Know the impact of your own experience with sexual trauma on a potential encounter with a fellow survivor. Projection is real.

Take care of yourself. Survivors can be retraumatized at any moment.

8

Feeling Silenced on Social Media? It Is Normal

Unfortunately, society often compares and measures the sexual trauma of individuals to some made-up standard. It is an improper use of power. Warped cultural ideologies, understandings, and biases concerning sexual violence rooted in ignorance and mistrust of people's narratives have caused further pain to survivors of sexualized violence.

The media, social media, and in-person conversations are full of instances in which one person's sexual trauma is viewed as inferior or minimized compared to a more horrible form, whatever that person determines it to be. These misconceptions are attempts to control the conversation. To control how one speaks about and responds to issues of sexual assault. And unfortunately, it is working.

I know this because I have allowed social media outlets to influence the way in which I not only respond to sexual violence but also whether I speak about mine. Social media has been flooded with survivors telling about their sexual trauma both before and after the wake of the #MeToo movement, an important movement that has provided resources for many survivors (as I stated earlier).

I cannot count the times that people began speaking up about their own sexual trauma on social media. Various outlets were flooded with debates and conversations and people "sounding the alarm." Detailed experiences were conveyed in technicolor and 3-D. Thankfully, many folks began their posts with a caution: "Trigger warning."

Because of the response *"I'm just glad you weren't raped,"* I felt that I had nothing to contribute to the conversation. I was sizing up my sexual trauma against those of other survivors. Not only did I feel silenced and put in my place in case I thought I actually went through something, I also allowed the church leader's remarks to dictate how I would engage conversations about sexual trauma.

I attempted to enter the conversation, but each account I read included surviving *rape*, which, because of the remark I heard in my personal conversation, I took as the supreme act of sexual violation. There was nothing worse than rape. It made me feel like my sexual trauma was insignificant. A scratch compared to a stab wound to the jugular.

As if playing double-dutch, I rocked back and forth, waiting for the right moment to enter the conversation, but I was afraid of being smacked by the "rope of disregard." I remained a bystander to the dialogue because I wondered,

What would I add to the conversation? Do I really have anything to say? Will they take me seriously? Will they silence me too?

So instead of engaging in the dialogue by sharing my experience, I made supportive comments like "I am praying for you" or "I am so sorry you experienced this." What happened to me remained with me and the few people to whom I "sounded the alarm." It turned into a dirty little secret. One that was too *insignificant* to name. And yet the irony is that it has *huge* effects for all the insignificance that I try to ascribe to it.

I was afraid.

I could not handle not being supported by the folks in my little world I chose to tell my story to. Social media is another ball game! What if I share what happened to me, and someone says that what I went through ranks low in terms of the level of severity? I do not know how I would respond to that. It would hurt, I am sure. I cannot even image what women who tell their experience on national television feel.

And yet, I have to tell myself—and I am telling you—that we have every right to engage in conversation regarding sexual trauma on social media (and beyond). No matter the details of our horrific experience. No matter what someone has said to us to discount our truths. No matter how unsure we are about where we land on the supposed "scale" of sexual trauma. There is no such scale. Resist it!

You have agency. You get to decide whether you will share your truth on social media. And either choice is the right choice. If you choose to tell your story on this virtual medium, do it being prepared to ignore any and all comments that seek to relegate your experience or silence your voice. And if you choose not to share your truth on social media, it does not mean that you are not brave. It does not lessen the gravity of your account. You do not need validation from online family, friends, or strangers. It is simply your choice.

Stand firm. Hold on to your truth. No matter what. Speak or don't. The choice is yours. Do what is best for you.

9

Know Your Limits: Refer. Refer. Refer!

I once heard a professor use the phrase, "I have reached the edge of my ignorance regarding that subject." I thought it was the most clever way of saying the three-word phrase children often accompany with a shoulder shrug: "I don't know."

When it comes to helping a survivor of sexual violence, we may not know what to do. We may be caught off guard when approached with someone's trauma. We may be at a loss for words. Like a deer in headlights, we may be paralyzed by the trauma we have just heard or the trauma that we see by looking at a survivor.

Do not wing it. Do not make stuff up as you go.

If there is any time for you to admit that "you've reached the edge of your ignorance," say so. Swallow your pride if that is what is keeping you from admitting your lack of knowledge around this topic, and tell the survivor the truth. Keep it simple: I don't know.

If you are a caregiver who is also a survivor, perhaps you might think about your own experience and what *you* needed when you "sounded the alarm." Remember that each survivor is also a unique individual. Although you both may have experienced sexual trauma, it does not mean that you "understand." Please do not say this. Details matter. A person's ability to deal with trauma matters. A person's circle of support, or lack thereof, matters. As discussed earlier, your own experience with sexual trauma impacts your encounter with a fellow survivor. This may be in a positive or negative way. At the very least, you may realize the importance of listening, validating (not comparing), and then determining *with the survivor* any next steps that they would like to take. Nevertheless, whether you are a survivor yourself or not, be clear on what you can and cannot handle.

You may say something like, "I am here to be a good listener, but you need more than what I can give you." Or, "I have not been trained to handle trauma such as yours." Or, "I have no idea what to do or say, but let us figure this out together." (See chap. 15.)

The point of this intentionally brief chapter is to tell you that the encounter with a survivor who has come to you to "sound the alarm" is not your opportunity to "play therapist." Real lives are at stake!

If you do not already have resources a survivor may need based on your conversation about them, get them. Gather the contact information for certified therapists, sexual assault crisis centers, medical doctors, friends, and the like, to name a few. Do not be embarrassed by your lack of knowledge. Put your pride aside.

Know your limits. And when you do not know:

Refer. Refer. REFER!

10

Avoid the Use of "Christian Band-Aids"

I begin this chapter with a poem I wrote on June 10, 2015.

"Christian Band-Aids"

"Weeping may endure for a night,
But joy comes in the morning!"
But I sit here struggling in my angst
And a new day is a-dawnin'
"Everything happens for a reason."
"It's all in God's plan."
But it's hard for me to divinize
suffering. I'm sorry. I just can't.
"All things work together for good . . ."
You know how that is finished.
And instantly whatever I am going through
is supposed to diminish?
Why? O why dear sisters and brothers,
do you make remarks like these?
Applying Scripture like a Band-Aid
with no balm for my dis-ease?
You don't listen to my pain.

Make no time to hear my thoughts.
Do not see the tears forming.
Care no mind that I'm distraught.
At least that's how it feels
when you apply a Christian Band-Aid.
I understand your motives may be good.
Your intentions begin from the heart.
The Scripture you quote is "good for my soul."
I believe that's where you start.
But can I ask you to back up a bit,
Just take a moment to see
That all I need from you right now
is to acknowledge my humanity?
I am in pain. I am hurting.
I have sorrow deep within.
I lack the energy to hope.
I do not know where to begin.
I just need someone to listen.
I just need someone who's there.
Not to fix my situation
Or to "God-talk me to care."
But to sit down in my presence.
To be quiet and let me be.
To let me rant about injustice,
What's not fair, or "Lord, Why me?"
Without interruption or instruction,
About how Christ paid it all,
About how we as Christians suffer,
About how sin came with the fall,
About how God gave up God's Son,
so that we all might live.
About how we as Christians
are supposed to forgive.
About how suffering brings perseverance,
About how troubles don't last always,
About how God's timing is not ours,
And how God turns our darkest nights into days!
I know you mean well.
I know you want to assist.
But this instant application of God's Word—
Please resist.

Until you've heard my truth.
Until you've acknowledged my pain.
Walked a mile in my shoes,
Actually experienced what I'm saying.
Asked me what I need
Or how you can help me, *if* you can.
And don't get mad if I tell you to back off.
"Talk to the hand!"
And then maybe . . . just maybe . . .
It won't feel like you're applying
a Christian Band-Aid.

★★★

I told her what he did to me. The more I spoke, the more freaked out she became. At least that is what I surmised by the look on her face. When I was finished, she looked lost. Like she didn't know what to say. At one point, I thought I would have to give her an out. "I am alright. I just thought you should know." Because I had no idea what she was thinking, I also thought that giving her an out would also save me from whatever was going to come from her mouth. She looked so distraught.

However, before I got a chance to utter my thoughts, her face lit up. A lightbulb must have gone on in her head because she kind of smiled. She held up one finger to signify she needed a minute, picked up her phone, and after a few taps she read to me the following:

First Corinthians 10:13 (NRSV) states, "God is faithful, and he will not let you be tested beyond your strength, but with the testing he will also provide the way out so that you may be able to endure it."

When she finished, I said, "Are you saying that I went through this because God was testing me?!" She did not respond, but she did find another passage.

Psalm 30:5 (KJV) says, "Weeping may endure for a night, but joy cometh in the morning."

She looked so satisfied with herself. She had found the answer to my problem. By uttering Scripture, she had gotten me one step closer to healing. I was going to be just fine because God is testing me; God knows how much I can bear, and the good news is that in the morning . . . !

I wanted to snatch her phone and throw it with all my might into the wall!

***

Christian Band-Aids. That is what I call them.

They are useful but do not heal. They are the words of God, but sometimes they function as Band-Aids. They cover up our wounds while *whatever else* we have applied to it does the healing. Band-Aids are useful because they provide a protective covering of our wounds.

Scripture *alone* does not heal. I believe that Scripture provides guidance for Christians with regard to living a faithful life and for attaining salvation. However, it does not provide magic words. This is what the woman in my encounter wanted to give me: magic words. Using Scripture as the sole form of assistance or aid to a survivor of sexual assault also does not work.

You are simply haphazardly slapping on a Christian band-aid to an oozing, growing wound.

When all she did was quote verses from the Bible to me, I got upset. Even her choice of texts was disturbing!

When she quoted 1 Corinthians 10:13, my initial response was, *"Are you saying that I went through this because God was testing me?!"*

I interpreted her use of that verse as her saying that my sexual trauma was a horrific event that God allowed—maybe even orchestrated—to test my faith. *This is a bit dramatic and over the top, don't you think?* I do not believe this is true. I *refuse* to believe this is the case. For the sake of my relationship with God, I *can't* believe this.

A God of love does not do this! I do not believe God is the author of my sexual assault, nor do I believe that God wants me to undergo such emotional turmoil *just to test my faith.* The God I serve does not want me to go through anything like that at all. At. All.

A more common rendition of the second part of that same verse is, "God does not give us more than we can bear." It's also troubling. At the time, I did not feel that I could bear the pain and shame and anger that I was experiencing. It was consuming me. It was suffocating me. It paralyzed me. It was too much! It was indeed *more than I could bear.* Because such trauma is too much to bear is precisely the reason that survivors need good caregivers to help release some of the burden.

Using Scriptures for the purpose of healing someone who

experiences a form of trauma in efforts to make them feel better *without anything else to accompany it* is simply applying Christian Band-Aids. Yes, I am an ordained minister, but I realize Scripture alone is not enough! Scripture by itself, with no further measures of care and comfort, and no other resources such as a therapist or medical professional, is just a set of words. This is Pastoral Care 101! When a minister goes to visit someone who is sick, do they read Scripture and then leave? No. At least they should not. It takes more—much more. Ministers bring listening, presence, and more.

The second Scripture text that she thought she was helping me with is one that I cringe at hearing. "Weeping may endure for a night, but joy comes in the morning" (Ps 30:5). When she said this to me, I thought, *Really? Because when I woke up this morning, there was no joy except maybe for the first few seconds when the reality of my sexual trauma did not re-emerge in my mind.* I wept all night. I weep all day. Joy escapes me. It is nowhere near my grasp. It is so far out of my reach that I no longer see it as attainable.

Of course, there are those who will say that joy is different from being happy. (*Insert head-slap emoji here.*) They will say to you until you are blue in the face that happiness is fleeting, but joy—the joy that comes from faith in God—is always there. To me, and potentially to other survivors, this explanation, this reasoning is not sound. In fact, it has the opposite effect of what its intended use may be. It hurts.

The notion that joy is always present if one has faith in God is also false logic. Psalm 30 says that weeping is real and enduring. The "Band-Aid" logic that joy is the only thing that is real is not at all what the Psalm says. Additionally, this Psalm is helpful for those who find themselves living in joy post-weeping, but not for those still weeping! Context matters!

Unfortunately, I have heard more than one person say to me that *joy comes in the morning.* I had the same reaction and response each time. One time, however, the Scripture-spewer refused to back down. She had what she thought was a comeback.

I told her, *"Joy did not come in my morning."*

She said, *"Well, you know that a thousand years to the Lord . . ."*

I stopped her and walked away. I could not hear anymore! She began citing 2 Peter 3:8 (NRSV), "But do not ignore this one fact, beloved, that with the Lord one day is like a thousand years, and a thousand years are like one day." So now she was explaining that our time is not the same as the Lord's. I had to stop thinking of "human time" and think about "divine time." *Whatever.*

Whatever healing powers she thought the words from that sacred text were supposed to have fell flat. The only thing this second Scripture did was upset me further. All it did was make me question whether Scripture could be *good* and/or *effective* in this situation. All it did was make me want to stay away from Christians!

The fact that her use of Scripture did nothing for me shook me to my core. God's Word as ineffective? That is blasphemy!

Right? But when she said those verses to me, it didn't *do* anything. I did not feel better. I did not feel any kind of relief. Growing up in church, I constantly heard that when trouble comes or when we need comfort, to seek it from the Word of God. *Hmm.*

In retrospect, I get it. As a person of faith who wants to provide comfort to a survivor of sexual assault (who may or may not be a believer), you may attempt to do that by sharing Scripture. Perhaps, as the words of the survivor began to enter your mind and turn into pictures and images of the horrific encounter, you may try to find solace not only for yourself but also for the individual who has suffered. You are reaching for something to say. Something to make them feel better. Something to ease, if not take away, their pain. Words fail you . . . *ahhh*, but Scripture . . .

In my experience, the citing of Scripture did not help me. Not by itself. I am not saying that it will not help *any* survivor. Just not me. I am also not saying that Scripture should not be used. What I *am* saying is that if you feel the need to cite Scripture, first ask the survivor if they want to hear it. And know that more often than not, if you cite Scripture as a means of comfort or cure *without* any other form of assistance, all you have done for the survivor is apply a "Christian Band-Aid."

Again, I am not diminishing or rejecting the use of Scripture when providing comfort. However, it should not be the first thing out of your mouth in response to hearing about a survivor's sexual trauma, nor should it be the only form of care provided.

As survivors, we need to know that we have been heard. That we are believed. That another flesh-and-blood hearer and now possessor of our trauma can sit in the utter darkness with us and be with us. To let us know that we are not alone. And to help us out of the dark pit in which we find ourselves, even if you need to call in reinforcements, that is, professional help. We need to know that you will be with us during our time of need.

If we request scripture to be read, then by all means, go for it.

Or, once you have listened and validated our stories, offered comfort and compassion, then ask if they want you to read some verses of comfort for them. Do not be offended if they say, "No." Do not be taken aback or become argumentative if a believer says they do not want to hear anything from the Bible. If they are anything like me, they may be angry with God, wondering why God allowed their sexual trauma to happen.

Theodicy, which includes wrestling with why bad things happen to good people, especially believers, becomes a struggle. I wanted no part of anything that was associated with God. Not the church. Not church folk. And not Scripture. I felt that God had turned God's back on me, so I turned my back on God.

As you will read in chapter 14, "Human Error and Church Terror: Healing the Broken Relationship with God," when a believer is sexually assaulted "in the church" (in all the various ways I describe in the introduction), to read Scripture when they come to you to "sound the alarm" may compound the trauma.

When sexual violence happens at the hand of a church leader or a church member, Scripture merely complicates the already difficult and conflictual feelings. When a caregiver cites Scripture in this instance, it feels like they are siding against the survivor by using precisely the weapons that are often part of the assault in the first place. There are predators in the church who assault folks because they feel it is their divine right. In their minds, a survivor's proper response is to *physically* care for the church leader who provides for their *spiritual* needs. Citing Scripture, then, may have the opposite effect of what a caregiver intends: instead of soothing us, it further hurts us. As a caregiver, you may want to remind us that God is with us, when all we are wondering is:

God, where were you?

Dear Fellow Survivor . . .

When you "sounded the alarm," did someone immediately cite Scripture to you? My guess is that if you do not believe in God, you probably wondered why this person chose to read the Bible to you. *This is not a matter of conversion. Are you suggesting that if I believed in God, this would not have happened to me? Certainly this cannot be what you are proposing!*

If you are a survivor who also believes in God, you may still ask the same question: *Why is this person reading Scripture to me now? I just finished telling them about my sexual trauma, and the best they can do is read the Bible to me? I know the Bible. I believe in God's Word, but those words are failing me right now! Please tell me this is not all they are going to do.*

For many survivors who are also believers, when we experience sexual trauma and "sound the alarm," we initially just want to be heard. We want to know that someone believes us. We want to know that the person we went to for help will *do something*. Not just quote Scripture.

Post-assault, a survivor's relationship with God may not be as strong as it used to be. Questions about God's sovereignty and power come into play. We wonder why God did not stop the assault from happening. We wonder, *Why us?*

If you asked those questions to another Christian, you may have heard the response, *"Why not you? Even Jesus suffered, and he is God's Son."* I know that is not helpful. As much as I wish it were the case, I know that Jesus's suffering and death does *not* mean that we will not suffer. It is extremely problematic and harmful, however, to suggest that just as Jesus's suffering was necessary, so is ours if we are to be Christ-like. (*I always did have a strong dislike for 1 Peter 2.*)

When you say, "They sexually assaulted me!" all you want to hear is, something like, "I am so sorry you experienced that." Not "Jesus suffered too." Or, "God is just testing you." Or, "God will not give you more than you can bear." Or, "Weeping may endure for a night, but joy comes in the morning."

Am I right?

Or perhaps I am thinking about this all wrong. People of faith have multiple responses to the use of Scripture quotations in this context. Some find them helpful. Scripture reminds them that God is with them *even as they* deal with the effects of their sexual trauma. Some want to completely reject Scripture, its authority, or its usefulness for this situation.

Scripture that tries to gloss over suffering, such as those that the woman mentioned to me in our encounter, are completely unhelpful. Scripture that draws the compassionate, loving, merciful God into a protective, accepting relationship with a survivor may be more helpful.

Maybe it is a matter of one's faith. I am the first to say that my faith wavers. I do not claim to be strong in my faith at all times, *especially during tough times.* I am very aware of this. Hearing Scripture in times of suffering does not help me, even as an ordained clergyperson and a Scripture scholar. I am being honest here.

Nevertheless, you may be just the opposite. You may need to hear Scripture because you have nothing else to cling to. Your faith is hanging on by its teeth, so you need to be reminded that God is with you. You may even rely on the faith of others until yours is strong enough. I have had to do that several times.

If someone begins to cite Scripture to you, and you do not wish to hear it, stop them. You do not have to listen to it. If they begin to quote verses from the Bible, and you are open to it, welcome it. My caution to you, however, is that you not allow the caregiver to use Scripture as a Band-Aid. Do not let them read the Bible to you without doing anything else, *unless* that is the sole reason you approached them.

Be your own advocate. It may be tough to continue fighting for what you need. You probably already used most of your strength "sounding the alarm." You do not have to entertain a debate about the use and importance of Scripture. Tell the caregiver, *"There is a time to talk, and a time to shut-up!"* (My paraphrase of Eccl 3:7b.)

Christian Band-Aids are not useful unless they are used with some form of balm or healing ointment. We do not need caregivers to "cover" our wounds, especially when we have ripped the Band-Aid off to "sound the alarm." *"Look! Look at what they did to me. Hear what happened to me!"*

Scripture can have a place in the survivor-caregiver encounter. Just not by itself. As survivors, we need more than a Band-Aid. We also need balm, that is, help in the form of a therapist, a crisis counselor, a person of the law, a shoulder to cry on . . . whatever we survivors say we need.

Ask for what you need.

Dear Caregiver . . .

Just because a survivor is also a believer, it does not mean that we want to hear Scripture at the time of our encounter—or at all, for that matter.

Citing Scripture may be your go-to because words of comfort may fail you. However, know that this may have an adverse effect. The survivor may feel like you are brushing them off, or you may have made their spiritual wound worse than what it was. *Where was God?*

If you are unsure if the reading of Scripture would be welcomed, just ask. It is bad form to simply assume that a survivor of faith wants or even *needs* to hear God's Word in any encounter you may have. This is not the time to beat a survivor over the head with Scripture. It is also not the time to graciously place a Christian Band-Aid on their wound either.

As I said earlier, just the reading of Scripture is not enough.

If you do not know what to do, be transparent, and tell the survivor that. Tell them that you wish you could do more, but all you can think of is to read Scripture, and you do not know if that would prove helpful to them. (Wait for their reply.)

If the survivor wants to hear Scripture, first ask them if they have something in mind. It may be their grandmother's favorite passage that brings them comfort. It might be God's vengeance as found in Revelation. It might be the narrative of Jonah. They may want to escape into the belly of a fish (despite not having a task to do from God). Whatever they want to hear, even if it makes no sense to you, read it. This is not a Bible study. A survivor might not want to hear your interpretation of the passage read. If they selected it, I am sure they already have an interpretation in mind.

If a survivor wants to hear something from the Bible but does not know which text, might I suggest that you avoid the ones I talked about earlier, for the reasons I also explained.

Perhaps select a text where someone other than Jesus deals

with pain, shame, or trauma and how they dealt with it. Share a passage of an individual who struggled with their faith.

Another option, which may be tougher for you, would be to choose a text that impels you to sit with the survivor in their pain. Try reading the lament passages found in the book of Psalms. There are plenty. For example, "Do not be silent, O God of my praise . . . They reward me evil for good, and hatred for my love . . . Help me, O Lord my God!" (Ps 109:1, 5, 26).

The bottom line is that Scripture can be helpful if requested by a survivor *and* if accompanied by another form of care. We are taught that God's words are powerful, and yet a survivor struggles with the lack of powerful action from God. *If God, then why . . .*

Do not apply Christian Band-Aids.

They don't stick.

11

Avoid Societal Assumptions. They Evoke Self-Blame.

She meant well. I think.

Months after I "sounded the alarm" the first few times, I took a chance and told a trusted friend about my sexual assault. At the time, I think we were having a conversation about something that was posted on social media regarding the #MeToo movement.

When I told her my truth, she gasped and said, "Oh no! How old were you?!"

***

"*How old were you?*" That was the first thing she asked me after exclaiming, "Oh no!" I was not expecting that question. After she said, "Oh no!" I expected her to say something like, "*I am so sorry that happened to you. Did you get the support you needed? Are you okay now? What can I do?"* Instead she asked how old I was.

How old was I? How old?! Does it matter? Does a younger age make the offense that much worse? Perhaps it does to her. Maybe thinking of a child experiencing what I did is unfathomable for her. For many, actually. That is, if we let societal assumptions prevail.

To me, my age was a non-factor. It did not matter how old I was. It did not matter whether I had already entered the stage where I could get pregnant. What gives?!

When she asked me that question, it shocked me. I may have hesitated for a few seconds, but I told her that I was in my early twenties. I do not remember verbatim what her response to that was, but I think it was something along the lines of, *"Oh. Well, I mean I am still sorry you went through that."*

As I mentioned above, she was a trusted friend at the time of our conversation. She still is. However, this does not mean that she is not prone to saying something that comes from a good place but still had an adverse effect on me. Most people do not know what to say in response to someone talking about their sexual trauma.

Notice that I did not refer to our encounter as me "sounding the alarm." Instead, I referred to it as a conversation in which I told her what happened to me. At this point, the people to whom I needed to "sound the alarm" had already been told. I was in counseling with a certified therapist working through things. I was not looking for her to assist me with anything. I did not need her to come to my aid. I did not need her to intervene on my behalf in any way. I told her because we were discussing the topic. I felt I had something to add.

When she asked about my age, I was taken aback, but I still think she meant well. I say this because not only was she always there for me, but she made her presence known to me even more after the conversation. I did not ask her for more attention. Yet she asked to spend more time with me. I had not asked her to help me with anything. Yet over time she repeatedly asked if I needed anything and if I was doing okay. She took my emotional temperature when the thermostat of the mistreatment of sexual assault survivors and their truths were running high.

She was there. She has been a blessing to me ever since—even as I write this book.

Therefore, I do not think she was *intentionally* passing judgment or making a point when she asked my age at the time of my sexual assault. I do not think that was it at all. Did she want to get more information? Perhaps. Honestly, I did not allow myself to analyze my conversation with her too much because I value her as a friend, and I do not think she meant any harm.

Nevertheless, hearing that question still hurt.

It took me aback. And between the time she had asked that question to the moment I answered her, I had already fired off a stream of questions in my head:

My age? My age?!

Why does it matter?!

If I was a child, does it make my trauma worse somehow?

If I was older than seventeen, does it implicate me in my own assault?

Are you asking because you want to know if I was capable of stopping it?

Why? Why? Why?!

I did not voice any of this to her. I simply answered her, "I was in my early twenties." But after that, I shut down. I no longer wanted to engage in this or any conversation at that time. I had disconnected. I felt silenced. I felt confused by her motives at that point in time. The history of our friendship was forgotten. I needed to leave and process. So I did.

She must have felt a change in my disposition, especially with the abrupt way I ended the conversation and decided to leave. Before I departed, she said, "I'm so sorry." We hugged and each went our own way.

Being asked, "How old were you?" in a conversation about sexual assault is not a good feeling. It feels like the validity or severity of my sexual assault is being quantified. Because I was older than the legal age of an adult, then what? I could have protected myself? I could have made better decisions? I should have been able to see the type of person my assailant was?

The number of questions I asked myself was endless! When I was asked about my age at the time of my sexual assault, it evoked a heck of a lot of self-doubt. Self-hatred did not take long to follow. Maybe I could have . . . Perhaps I should have . . . If I had . . . , then he . . . Did I fight or just brace until it was over? Should I have been old enough to . . . ?

What does age have to do with it?

Absolutely nothing! Sexual assault is sexual assault. At any age. The only thing that I can think of where this matters is in terms of the law. Even then, there are penalties and laws in place for every age, right? Again, not my expertise.

"How old were you?" Again, we are back to the socially established and maintained hierarchies of pain and culpability with regard to sexual assault. The power dynamics at play in terms of cultural understandings of what one is capable of, and what age deserves the most sympathy, make it difficult for those of us who are survivors to share our truths. We question ourselves, wondering if our sexual trauma will be discounted or dismissed.

Let me be clear: I am not dismissing or lessening trauma experienced by children at all. I think that is horrible as well. What I am arguing here is that no one should be asked how many years they have been alive when they have experienced sexual violence.

With regard to sexual assault, there is no age range that determines how much one has suffered, how much a person *could have* done to prevent it, or how much attention and help a person requires and/or deserves. One's age does not equal one's agency. How old you are does not determine how much you can do or could have done to protect yourself.

Every survivor, no matter their age, deserves help without scrutiny. I understand that questions need to be asked in terms of gathering information in an investigation; however, I am uncertain as to how one's age might apply here. Asking a survivor their age makes us question ourselves. It silences us until we have come to terms with having been asked that question or until someone else validates our truth.

Societal assumptions do not help survivors. In fact, they make us feel worse.

Dear Fellow Survivor . . .

Am I right? Do you agree that asking the age of someone who has been sexually assaulted implies that their age determines how much agency they had in their own violation? To stop it, that is? Does it not cause self-doubt to take root?

Perhaps no one asked you how old you were when you shared your truth. Maybe you heard something like the following:

"Were you drinking?"

"Did you watch your drink to make sure no one put anything in it?"

"What were you wearing?"

"Did you flirt?"

"Why didn't you use your strength to stop it? You're strong."

"But you're a dude! You didn't like any of it? Maaaaan, if that was me, I'd . . ."

"What about all of those self-defense classes you've taken?"

All of these phrases and questions are rooted in societal assumptions that have determined how a person is supposed to act and be capable of based on their age, anatomical makeup, size, and more. These are unfair assumptions to make. All they do is place the blame on us as the survivor. We begin to question every move we made when our sexual trauma occurred.

Although the above statements were said, what we hear is:

"Why were you drinking? You know it lessens your ability to make good decisions."

"We always talked about not leaving your drink unattended. What were you thinking?"

"You should not have worn those fishnet stockings. You know they are tempting."

"Why were you flirting with them if you didn't want to do anything further?"

"What's the point of lifting all those weights if you still can't protect yourself?"

"Come on, man. We're dudes! 'No' doesn't apply to us. You know this!"

"And to think, you took all of those self-defense classes. What was the point?"

This must stop!

We have to do our best not to internalize how these questions and statements make us feel. I know it is hard, but we must try. We also need to be more verbal about correcting these misconceptions based on these troublesome societal assumptions. They are lies!

No matter if we were drinking. No matter our clothing. No matter if we flirt. No matter if we are strong. Or a man. Or know a form of self-defense.

OUR SEXUAL TRAUMA IS NOT OUR FAULT!

We are not to blame!

I know it is hard to keep self-doubt at bay. I deal with it daily. I even feel bad when I am triggered. *Why does this still bother me? Am I not strong enough to not let this bother me?* It is a constant battle. I cannot say that I have it all figured out. I still have self-doubts. I still "suck my teeth" at myself for not seeing the signs (see chap. 1). But as I assert in that chapter, it is not my fault. No matter what anyone says. No matter what society puts forth as standards or requirements for how one deals with sexual assault, please:

Do not let it undermine your feelings.

Do not doubt yourself one bit.

Remember that what happened to you was not your fault.

You did not do anything to provoke it.

Your age does not make you accountable for any part of it.

Your size does not make you better fit to stop it.

None of these things determine your pain, participation, or ability to prevent the horrible sexual trauma that you experienced. None of it.

I give you permission to release yourself from societal standards and understandings about sexual assault.

I give you permission to claim your voice and know that your truth is just as important as anyone else's *regardless of age.*

I give you permission to trust that you did anything and everything you needed to do in order to survive your assault.

YOU SURVIVED.

Dear Caregiver . . .

A survivor chose you because they either trust you, or because you are a professional who can help them in a particular way regarding their sexual assault. I understand that during the encounter, you may need to ask questions. You may need additional information. However, as I have said numerous times, first just LISTEN. Then VALIDATE the survivor's truth. Do not make any comparisons. Take note, and take hold of your own feelings regarding your own trauma if you are a survivor yourself so that they do not negatively impact your encounter with a fellow survivor.

Do not subscribe to societal assumptions in order to inform the way you engage with a survivor. If they are an adult, their age does not matter. If they are younger, there may be additional laws in place. However, whether the survivor is an adult or a child, that person deserves the same amount of attention, care, and assistance.

The same applies to one's sexual parts. A man can be sexually assaulted by a woman. He will more than likely, however, have trouble being believed because of the notion that a man—a "real" man—would not only have been able to prevent a woman (supposedly a physically "weaker being") but also that he would have enjoyed it *even if he was roofied*. This thinking is problematic. It maintains a stereotype about what a "real" man is and also prevents men who have been sexually assaulted to "sound the alarm." They are embarrassed. They are ashamed. But they need help too!

Making judgments based on how a survivor looks, what

sexual body parts they have, whether or not they party too much, and so on is offensive. It is wrong. It is not caring. And it only aggravates their pain, multiplies the effects of their trauma, and silences them. They no longer want to share their truth because they do not want to be rejected, judged, or ridiculed.

Questions such as the ones mentioned above make it seem like a survivor's sexual trauma was in some way justified. That we brought it upon ourselves. That if we were just a little more careful, then . . . Maybe we tempted them when we wore that dress, those nice slacks . . .

Society has created and maintained assumptions that work against survivors. Do not subscribe to them. Do not make judgments about a survivor or their truth because of them. Help us destroy them. The factors that I mentioned here (age, sexual body parts, strength, etc.) do not begin to cover all of them. There are plenty more. My list is not exhaustive.

So when approached by a survivor to hear their truth, listen. Validate. Make no comparisons. Ask questions. And think.

We need you to think before you speak.

You will make mistakes, and that is okay so long as you own them, apologize for them, and learn from them. We need you. We need you more now than ever.

12

There's a Lot behind a S.M.I.L.E. (Simply Making It Look Easy)

I told her that I needed to talk to her. That it was important. I told her that "relationships will be destroyed."

She told me that no matter what, she would be there for me. No matter what, she would support me.

A week later, we met, and with teary eyes and quivering lips, I told her.

Everything.

The reason I told her "relationships would be destroyed" is because she knows the man who sexually assaulted me. She is close with him and his family.

I needed her to be there for me.

I needed her to hear my truth.

I needed her to choose me . . . over him. This proved to be problematic because breaking a relationship with him meant losing her relationship with his family. In retrospect, it was not fair of me to ask her to reject the innocent because of him. I did not realize I was doing this at the time. Retrospection brings out the complexities of situations like this. It still hurt, however, because I lost her in the process.

She got teary-eyed the more I talked. She shared some things about herself that are hers to tell.

She had a few "ah-ha" moments about things she'd heard or seen with respect to him and his relationship with other young girls. About gifts he'd bought them. About having visits in his home. Taking them to plays, museums, expensive dinners. (All of that sounded very familiar.)

She told me she believed me. She told me she was glad that I confided in her. We ended up feeling closer. Correction: I felt closer to her. But after a couple of weeks, I realized I was wrong.

A week went by. Two weeks went by. I still hadn't heard from her. Not a call. Not a text. Not a "How are you?"

Nothing. Abso-freaking-lutely nothing.

So I reached out to her via text. "Hey. I'm just checking in. I haven't heard from you."

Crickets.

A week later, I heard back from her. But it was far from what I expected. She'd had several conversations, one of which included a talk with him. The very man that touched me. The very man that violated me. The very man that I told her took advantage of me.

You would think that's a good thing, right? That she put him in his place. That she defended me. That she couldn't believe that he would do such a thing!

Nope. Nuh uh.

It didn't go down like that. At least not based on what she texted back.

"It couldn't have been that bad."

She texted, "It couldn't have been that bad!"

They talked about me.

I imagine her listening to him tell his side of what happened. I wonder if he told her everything. I wonder if his "story" comes even close to my version. I doubt it. Because what I got in response proved their discussion took a whole different turn.

After she said, "It couldn't have been that bad," she proceeded to tell me all of the things I was able to do with and for the man who assaulted me after he "so-called" (her words) touched me inappropriately. She then texted me what she and my assailant had worked out using his narrative as the historical truth and mine as the "fanciful re-creation."

The Molester Collective.

That is what I called them.

They "confirmed" that I wasn't a minor. That I was in my twenties, and so I could have stopped it if I wanted to.

"I knew better."

I braided his daughter's hair.

I attended events at his home.

I laughed at his jokes.

All of these things . . . and more.

She listed everything that I did with him that proved—without a shadow of a doubt—that what he did to me couldn't have been that bad.

She told me, "It couldn't have been that bad."

"That bad? That bad?!"

***

How dare she! How dare she type out all of the things that I did with, for, and near the man who sexually assaulted me? How does that, in any way, erase what he did to me? What if he had threatened me? What if I was afraid? What if??

What made it worse is that the list she texted me was a compilation that the two of them—my supposed "caregiver" and my assailant—thought of together! They compared notes. They put them in order of occurrence. They went back to add details and colors. They proofread.

As I said before, not everyone wants, or cares to be, *your* caregiver. I approached her under the assumption that she would be there for me. She never verbally said, "Yes, I will be that person." However, she initially said she believed me and that she was glad I confided in her. Nevertheless, her actions said unequivocally, "No!" Implicit assent to caregiving but without active follow-up is sometimes more damaging than rejection.

I could not accept this.

Together, they outlined my actions. She texted me the resulting list. Each conversation, each event, each memory that she recaptured was like a hard slap in the face. A kick in the gut and the head while I lay on the ground in a fetal position. They were relentless!

She didn't believe me. (Even though when it was just her and I, she said she did.)

She didn't believe it was *that traumatic.*

She "witnessed" me moving on. I was able to function *normally.* I was able to act as if nothing happened, so maybe nothing did happen; *if* it did, then it was not debilitating or as bad as I made it out to be. My run-of-the-mill, ordinary actions led her to believe that I was just fine. My coping mechanism became precisely her ammunition for dismissing me.

But there is a lot behind a S.M.I.L.E. (Simply Making It Look Easy).

I am sure that I made it look easy because, as I explained earlier, my brain was protecting me. I had no recollection of what he did to me. I was operating as if nothing happened. I do not know how soon after my sexual assault that I began to "forget." Years later, when I no longer resided in the same state, when the chances of seeing him lessened significantly, my brain was flooded with images, conversations, trauma.

At the time of my conversation with her, I was unaware of my "window of amnesia." As I mentioned earlier, this refers to when our brains function as our protectors by blocking out the traumatic events we have endured. I was not able to explain how my body protected itself. I was so confused! *"What happened to my memory? How was I able to do all of those things my onlookers graciously (insert sarcasm here) reminded me I did with, for, and around my assailant post-assault? I had to have been angry. I had to have remembered what he did to me. Right? Where did my memories go? How did I manage to do these things to the point that no one else suspected anything was wrong? Surely, there is a reasonable explanation for this!"*

When my brain compartmentalized my trauma—locked it away—it also took some other memories with it. This process of temporary amnesia to keep unwanted memories at bay also interferes with the making of new ones. I have pockets of time during my life that I cannot recall. It's like my brain time-warps through my life. The only evidence that I have of anything happening in my past is from the recollections of others that I trust, and from pictures. Lots and lots of pictures.

I wish I could recall those other memories—hopefully good ones. But those memories are a small price to pay for keeping that traumatic experience from my mind for so long, until my body knew I was ready for it to be released. Until I had what I needed, namely a therapist, a support system, and distance—a safe and secure environment to deal with it.

Looking back, I do not think it would have mattered if I were able to explain to her what a "window of amnesia" was. She had already decided. She had already outlined the ways I engaged with my assailant. Some things cannot be erased. Her further lack of support showed me that she would not be there for me. Disbelieved. Rejected. Abandoned. By someone I love.

Nevertheless, I am grateful. I am grateful that my body

protected me all those years. It still does. Retelling my truth to my therapist revealed that the entire incident has not been released. It has now been more than twenty years. As I mentioned earlier, I believe that whatever my brain is keeping buried is severely traumatic. Apparently, my brain does not think I am ready for full disclosure of what happened to me. I still do not know what happened to me in its entirety. A full recollection is still not available to me—thus the gaps in my retelling.

There is more. There is *definitely* more. I could work on accessing all of what happened. My therapist could help me unlock memories. She said "Yes" to this possibility. But I have said "No." *Definitely* not happening. Nope. Nuh uh. I am not ready. I shake my head repeatedly left to right like she is serving my memories on a platter, and I am deathly allergic to them. I am afraid. I am deathly afraid of what I will learn.

I am afraid. Not only of what else he did to me but also of how I will deal with the fact that there will be no recourse. There will be no justice served on my behalf.

Just like when I "sounded the alarm" to a mutual friend of ours, I imagine him walking away with a slick grin on his face saying, *"Yeah, you thought you had me."*

Nothing will happen *again.* Further evidence of my trauma would simply be a point of information. Just something else to haunt me. Something else to make me question my strength and my love of self. It would be a matter of devastation. A whole new string of what-ifs. And I cannot handle that right now. I cannot. I still struggle with what I *do* know.

Maybe one day I will be ready to do the work to unlock the rest of my trauma. But that day is not today. Nope. Not today. That day may never come. And I am okay with that.

Dear Fellow Survivor...

Are you "fakin' it till you make it"? Are you going through the motions, doing your everyday, normal activities? Are you smiling while you do it? *Simply making it look easy?*

When you "sounded the alarm," did the person you told doubt you? Did they second-guess what you told them? Did they give you a rundown of how you behaved since your sexual trauma? Did they even include the times when you acted "normal" or even nice around your assailant?

Perhaps you heard something like the following:

"But I never saw you cry."

"But you laugh and smile all the time."

"But you look *normal.*"

"But you waited so long to tell someone."

What are we supposed to say to these things? Might I suggest our responses be: *And? So? So what? Why does that matter? It does not negate what I told you!*

They. Have. No. Idea. Again, there is a lot behind a smile. On the outside, we may appear to be calm, but on the inside, there is a storm brewing. On the outside, we may appear cool and collected, but on the inside, we are simmering! On the outside, we may don a smile, but on the inside—oh, on the inside—we are scowling!

There is pain. There is shame. There is anger. There is

frustration from having our truths be questioned because of the way we try to continue to live! We are surviving! That is what they see, right?

And yet because we are determined not to give up, because we have decided to continue our routines, because we have chosen not to surrender to the negative emotions that at any moment can paralyze us and break us . . . *it could not have been that bad.*

When people discredit our pain, deny our trauma, or say something like what I heard, a humongous seed of self-doubt sets in. We begin to question ourselves. We begin to doubt our self-worth. For me, it was a downward journey into self-loathing, insecurity, and feelings I could not shake. Perhaps your inner inquisition after having heard "It couldn't have been that bad" or the like included the following:

"Why *did* I do those things after my assault?"

"How was I able to do those things?"

"I was angry. Right? I had to have been angry."

"Why did I live my life like 'business as usual'?"

"Are they right? Am I making more of this than it is?"

"Was it *trauma* or simply a misunderstanding?"

STOP.

Really. Just stop.

We have to stop doubting ourselves no matter how hard the task may be and no matter how convincing the "evidence" presented by others appears to be. What they say does not matter. Do not listen to them. No matter what they say, our sexual assault is not our fault.

IT IS NOT OUR FAULT!

No matter how many times you have to repeat this to yourself, do it. I have not figured out how to make that understanding stick. At times I still fall back into the feeling of self-doubt. I have not found the solution to stopping this cycle of uncertainty and self-loathing. So when that feeling rears its ugly head, I have to remind myself, "It is not my fault."

Saying these things to myself is not easy. It does not always work. It is not always immediate. But I get there . . . eventually. Only to have to repeat the process all over again.

Many of us did those things post-assault as a means of survival. We did those things because we perhaps felt no one would believe us anyway. We did those things to protect us from further violence from our perpetrators. We did those things because we did not want to feel our pain, and so we *needed* normalcy. We needed to recapture the self we had *prior* to the assault that changed everything. We needed us—the way we used to be.

Whatever you do to S.M.I.L.E. (Simply Making It Look Easy) post-assault is a survival strategy. I applaud you. I applaud you for not giving up on yourself. And I affirm your agency in making decisions about how to keep living, to keep surviving.

Live your life!

Dear Caregiver . . .

When you see a survivor smiling and having a good time, it does not mean that they are "over it." It does not mean that *"it couldn't have been that bad."* It does not mean that they are alright. It does not negate or lessen their truth. It may not make sense to you, but please take my word for it.

As a caregiver of a survivor, you need to be aware that there just might be a lot behind a survivor's smile. Just because we greeted you joyfully or are caught laughing does not mean that all is right and okay in our world. We still harbor thoughts of self-loathing, a constant feeling of being dirty, self-doubt, and more just below the surface.

And yet we smile. Why? For many reasons. Hopefully our smile is authentic because we are having a good moment! One of the dangers of caregivers knowing about our trauma—knowing the "behind the scenes" information—is that pity becomes the operative relational mode. *Oh look, they are smiling: How brave they must be!* The fact of the matter is that we are smiling because we are experiencing real joy in that moment. The pity party response does not always need to be enforced.

We also smile for the sake of our sanity; we need an optimistic mindset. Sometimes we need to pretend that all is right in our world. We smile because we do not want the extra attention. *What's wrong?* We smile because we know that folks don't really want to know—or cannot handle—our trauma. This is evident when folks ask how we are doing and then move on before we can even respond with a rote "Fine" or "Good." We smile because if our faces expressed our inner thoughts and turmoil, folks would "head for the hills."

I am not suggesting that you, as caregivers, go around questioning each and every smile you see. Rather, take a few minutes to make sure that a survivor's smile is authentic, *especially* if this person has already informed you about their sexual trauma. We may not want to unpack or unleash all of our feelings at that moment, but we may need you to follow up with us to schedule another more convenient time to check in.

Do not let our actions fool you into thinking that we are doing so well that you no longer tend to us. Check on us. Do not let our actions influence the way you engage us or respond to our requests for help, or if you wonder if what we went through was as bad as we said it was.

The phrase "Actions speak louder than words" does not always apply to a survivor. Investigate. Ask questions. *I'm just making sure that you are okay . . .* Often we as survivors *feel* forgotten and abandoned. This could be because we play the part of happy so well. We may *look* like we are content, doing better, and, dare I say, happy. But as evidenced by this chapter, *there is a lot behind a S.M.I.L.E.*

We are Simply Making It Look Easy.

But it is not.

13

Wounding Remarks Come from Wounded People

You may have heard it expressed this way: "Hurt people hurt people." It is so true. Here is why I think this is the case. It is my way of making sense of how a loved one was able to be so mean, so uncaring, so vindictive. I am not excusing her actions. I am trying to understand them.

In light of hearing *"It couldn't have been that bad"* and the inner struggles that resulted from it, I could not for the life of me understand why someone close to me could make such a hurtful, dismissive statement about my trauma. I just could not fathom it. Call me naive.

After that conversation, things took a turn for the worse. Hateful things were spewed back and forth between the two of us. One of those statements was, *"So what, he touched you!"* Yeah, she said that. I am also not proud of some of the things I said to her. To be honest, it felt good at the time.

Now? Not so much. It took five years—yes, *five years*—but we were able to have a civil conversation in which apologies were exchanged. Nevertheless, our relationship remains rocky—borderline nonexistent—and will never be the same. I share our encounter because there is a lesson to be learned.

In therapy I learned to step back and consider what may have been behind the retort, *"So what, he touched you!"* Perhaps elements of power and pain are at work here. That is, more often than not, when someone says something like that, it is uttered from a place of pain.

Perhaps the power she tried to exert over me by dismissing my sexual assault (*"It couldn't have been that bad"*) masks what she is really saying: *"So what, he touched you! Get over it. It happened to me too!"* This was her way of taking back the power that someone may have taken from her. She exerted power in a negative way because of her pain.

I am in no way excusing her actions. I am trying to understand them.

Thinking about her remarks coming from a place of pain, however, makes it sting *less* because it definitely still stings. Although it was wrong of her to speak such vitriol, I am trying to consider her own pain. Perhaps she was incapable of being there for me because no one was there for her. Projection is real. Her anger toward me may have had nothing to do with me, but I provided her with an opportunity she could not miss. It was time for her payback. She finally had an opportunity to get even, to let it out, albeit with the wrong person. Her anger was misplaced. Instead of being angry at her assailant, she misdirected it at me.

With the help of my therapist (*if you do not have one, please get one*), I was able to interpret her directed anger as projected pain. As I recounted my truth, I may have unlocked hers. Perhaps this is why she was unable to respond to me. Was she dealing with her own sexual trauma? Is that the reason I had to reach out to her after "radio silence" for a couple of weeks? Perhaps she had flashbacks. Perhaps she could smell the smells and recall the color and condition of the walls of when she was assaulted. Who knows if my truth forced her to deal with hers? What if the recollection of her own trauma snapped her back into her present reality with renewed pain and anger because no one helped her? Because she had to protect herself? She had to toughen up and make it through on her own. *"So what, he touched you!"* was the undercurrent of her narrative.

That was what she *said*. But what I was later able to imagine with the help of my therapist was a hurt little girl. I was able to see the little girl suffering alone and in silence. I imagine her saying, *"There's no one I can tell. They won't believe me. There's no one to help me. Why would they leave me with him? Do they not know what he does to me? Do they care?"*

I can see how a hurt little girl can grow into a woman who masked her pain with anger and toughness. I can see her emotions turn callous and cold. Sympathy became situational, that is, when it benefited her. I can understand her resolve to say she was not going to choose between me and the man who assaulted me (although she did by choosing his narrative over mine). Perhaps no one chose her. All of these things—over time—have tempered my anger, and at times caused my anger to topple over into sympathy.

Yep. I feel sorry for her. Isn't that something?

Dear Fellow Survivor . . .

People who utter sentiments like *"So what, they touched you!"* may be speaking from a place of pain. Nevertheless, what they are doing is assuming a certain posture of power to discount and discredit our stories. They have made themselves an authority in how to interpret our actions and may even be trying to script how we view and question ourselves as a result. They try to temper our cries and lessen or negate our pain by putting a negative spin on our attempt at survival, on our need for normalcy, on the days when we want to pretend our assault never happened. They want to unravel the reality of our ordeals. They want to dismiss the distress that we carry within us. They want to sever the sting of our violent experiences. All because of their own hurt.

Do not let them.

Do not let them question your truth. Do not let them instill doubt in your mind about the severity of what happened or the actions you took to function and survive despite them. Do not let them lessen or discount your pain.

Feel what you feel.

Our mode(s) of survival is part of our recovery. It is evidence of our strength. We do not have to explain it. And we do not need others to validate it.

If you are anything like me, you may need permission to do just that. You may need consent to continue striving for "normalcy" in your everyday life despite what others say. You may need authorization to take back the authority over how you interpret your actions and the choices you made post-assault. You just might need the clearance to cuss somebody out, create new ways of being, or come up with different strategies of coping.

YOU ARE HEREBY GRANTED PERMISSION.

GO.

BE.

DO.

Dear Caregiver...

Are you wounded? Are you a survivor who has yet to deal with your trauma? Have you responded in a harsh way to a fellow survivor because you felt slighted that you did not receive the help you needed, and this person *has the nerve* to request aid from you? Are you projecting your pain onto someone who does not deserve it?

Is this you? If so, please read chapter 7.

As fellow survivors, we need to embrace each other, not reject each other. Support one another, not cause further harm.

If you are wounded, please get the help you need. You

might even find what you need if you choose to journey together with a fellow survivor, as I discuss in chapter 15.

If you have not experienced this kind of trauma, listen to the survivor's truth without judgment. Validate it. Be a supportive presence to the survivor, and ask them in what way(s) you can be of assistance.

14

Human Error and Church Terror: Healing a Broken Relationship with God

"I miss you at church, Shanell. Everyone asks how you are doing. The Women's Guild asked me to see if you could preach for Women's Day this year. But I told them that your schedule is really busy. Do you think you will ever come back?"

"I'm not ready. Furthermore, the answer is 'No,' because he is still there."

***

My sexual trauma did not occur within the walls of the church, but it was a male church leader who violated me. A church leader who is a mentor to the youth, who serves in leadership roles in the church, who reads and interprets the Word of God from the pulpit . . .

From the pulpit. *That location matters.* It matters to me because of the visual it presents. He stands above the rest of us. He is positioned front and center. His frame is situated right behind the cross on the communion table, right in front of the very large stained-glass window depicting Jesus in the heavens. In the midst of all that beauty stood ugliness encased in human flesh. Smack dab in the middle of all that we deem holy was the most vile and sacrilegious person I have ever met. Right at the center of all that represented God's love stood a man I loathed.

And yet, he is a "man of God."

Heck, when he opened his mouth from the pulpit, he was the *voice of God!* Isn't the preacher supposed to represent God?

Can you imagine how it feels to see the person who sexually assaulted you preach from the pulpit? How would you feel knowing that even after you "sounded the alarm," your assailant would continue to be in some type of leadership role in the church? *He is still a church leader!*

He proclaims the Word of God even as he claimed ownership of my body on that day. The same hands that he uses to high-five the youth of the church, to turn the pages of the Bible, to rest on the shoulders of people being ordained for service . . . those very same hands made my skin crawl.

My sexual trauma may have occurred in a location other than the church, but he still remained a church leader in my eyes. Even in his home. *"Let your actions speak your faith,"* they say. Well, his actions had a lot to say that day.

His actions made me think that God makes mistakes. His actions told me that just because someone is a church leader does not mean that they will act Christ-like at all times. His actions told me that faith and faithfulness are two different things. Faith is what this church leader had in God. But he lacked faithfulness. He failed to show with his actions just what his faith in God was supposed to mean.

I was so angry and confused!

I attended the same church as the man who sexually assaulted me. I was going to the very same church where I would see the folks to whom I "sounded the alarm" and did nothing. Sunday after Sunday we greeted each other. We passed the peace of Christ. We sang hymns together. Read liturgies in unison. We praised God as one church. From the outside, the congregation looked like a unified, God-loving, God-praising entity, but the disjointedness and fragmented relationships therein suggest it was all an illusion.

Remembering and revisiting my days in that church messed me up. It messed me up bad. It put a cloud over all the good memories I had growing up in that church. It totally eclipsed the times when I would smile and laugh and hug the mothers of the church and kiss the little babies on their cheeks. I had forgotten about all of that . . . because of him, and because of those who rejected me and discounted my truth. No wonder my brain made the memory of That Day inaccessible. Locked away.

No wonder I was able to sit in my pew as he read the Scripture and proclaimed the Word. No wonder I did not jerk away when he laid hands on me with the other church leaders when I was ordained as an elder. No wonder I was able to receive his remarks of praise and congratulations when I accepted the call to ministry and eventually became a minister.

No wonder. I know I would have gone insane. I know I would have lost my mind. I would have lost weight. I would have lost my hair, or rather pulled it out. I would have bitten all of my nails down to the nub. I would have . . . *What wouldn't I have done?*

I am so grateful that I did not recall any of what he did to me until I no longer had to be in the same vicinity as him. I am so happy to have a community of support where I am now instead of sulking from the lack of care I received from those who I thought would be there for me.

I may no longer be in their presence, but the effects of what I went through have remained. Church folks hurt me. God's folks hurt me. God hurt me.

My theology got jacked up! My faith in God was nearly gone. I was so confused. I could not differentiate God from God's people anymore.

Church. Assault. Faith. Trauma. God. Sinners.

The profane and the sacred are blurred.

Before my assault, the church was a place of refuge. Afterward, it became a place to avoid. It once was a place to see the spirit move. It is now a place to see where danger lurks. It used to be a place to sing praises. Presently, it is a place where skepticism resides.

Before my assault, God was the great physician who heals. Now, God is Houdini—the magician who disappears.

Human error led to church terror.

Everywhere.

The lens through which I view God is blurry at best.

I do not want to hear Scripture because it has become tangled with suffering. The reading of God's Word is twisted with God's inability to protect and to provide comfort. My faith—that thing that compels me to read the Bible to inform and build on my relationship with God—is intertwined with the fear that God has forgotten and turned God's back on me.

I chuckle and twist my lips when hymns are sung in church about God's power and God's protection and how we live to praise. *"God's my rock?"* Umm, no. *"Thank you, Lord?"* For what? *"He said, 'Peace, be still'?"* Really? When? *"Jesus, you are the center of my joy? All that's good and perfect comes from you?"* But church folks come from you too, right God?

The worlds of the sacred and secular became blurred. The love I had for God before my memories came back filled me. Sure, I questioned God about some things. I grieved my maternal grandparents' death. But I always knew deep down that God loved me. I did not doubt that God would be with me through those hard times.

And then the scales fell from my eyes. What I thought about God was not clear to me anymore. When images of my sexual assault flashed in my mind, I asked God about God's whereabouts. When I think about the conversations and arguments I had with those to whom I "sounded the alarm," I wonder why God is not chastising them. I wonder why God did not soften their hearts. I wonder why God did not do something *through them for me!*

My God, My God, why has thou forsaken me? Me! The "good girl." I am the one who read the Bible every night. I told pursuers that you were my boyfriend. I was the loner, the one who never got invited to anything because I was different. I was "set apart" because of my love for God. I never hid my adoration of you. I sang solos in the choir. I preached what you told me to preach even when it made me feel vulnerable. I sat there in church on many evenings in meetings trying to figure out how we can do more for the community, how we can excite others in the congregation to get more involved. I went to seminary *for you.* I got a doctorate *for you.* I did it *for you, O God,* because I truly believe that is what you called me to do. To teach other pastors and church leaders about the New Testament so that they can go out and teach others.

I did it for you, God. And what did you do for me? (*This blinking cursor is telling.*)

Therein lies the root of my pain. I feel that God abandoned me. If God is so powerful, then . . . If God is all knowing, then . . . If God is everywhere, then . . .

WHY???

I am angry with God. And that is okay, because God knows anyway. My anger with God is transparent, and I believe God accepts that. What I cannot do, however, is pretend that I am not angry with God and perpetuate a myth from the pulpit. I am called to be a preacher and a teacher of Scripture, but working through my trauma has meant forsaking part of my call, which sets conditions for even more anger. *Thank you for the invitation, but unfortunately, I am unable to preach* . . .

I am skeptical of anything related to church and church folks. I do not put anything past church leaders. Some people have suggested that I attend a church with female church leaders. I laugh because I had only "sounded the alarm" to women. Look where that got me. Gender essentializing—that female leaders can help assault survivors heal better than male leaders—is one of the biggest myths out there about caregiving and ecclesiastical responses to sexual abuse.

My relationship with God is strained. It is rocky. However, I am beginning to work on that. I have been angry for over five years with God, with the church, and with church folks. I am exhausted. And I miss God. I miss the way we used to talk. The way God used to make me laugh. The way God would reveal things to me in unique ways. I miss feeling God's presence around me.

After five years, I am ready. No, I am not going to jump head-first into the pool of commitment and involvement in church. I do not even have a church home. Presently, I do not want one. I still do not trust the church. I do not want to be tied down to a community of people who will eventually have the opportunity to disappoint and hurt me. I know, I know—I cannot live this way. Not for long, anyhow. I know that no one is perfect. I know that being a part of a religious community has its benefits. And I enjoy them, but at my pace.

What is interesting is that my working on my relationship with God began in therapy, not in a church, and not with church folks. *Church is not the only space where God encounters and loves us!* In therapy, I am learning how to differentiate God from God's people. It seems as if that would be an easy task, but it is quite difficult. I know in my head that God and God's people are distinct entities, but in my heart it gets jumbled up.

God and God's people became jumbled together into one entity because they are tied together in the same emotions. Both God and God's people abandoned me, hurt me, disappointed me, and angered me. Both God and God's people are associated with church. And so I want nothing to do with church. Both God and God's people are involved with Scripture, and the words on those pages surely cannot be true, especially those pertaining to God's love.

I loved God, and I loved those church folk. And they hurt me. They let me down. They treated me wrong. They made me feel bad about myself. They made me doubt my truth. They made me question what love really was, and they made me take a closer look at our relationship. What did I miss? Had I read our relationship wrong? Perhaps I felt more for you than you did for me. I suspected everything and everyone—*especially* if they had anything to do with God or the church.

I am a work in progress. I am unlearning bad theology. I

internalized the idea that I must have done something wrong for God to let me experience such horrible trauma. This is one of the main theologies I am unlearning. As a result, I am learning to be intentional about who God is and how God is distinct from God's people. I have to be deliberate in remembering that those who read Scripture, teach the Bible, or preach from the pulpit may represent God, but they are not God. They are human, and thus they are sinful. Although they may interpret God's Word, it does not mean they are without fault. It also does not mean that they are the voice of God. For this reason, I must continue to read and study God's Word myself. *Test the spirits.*

Every day I am working to have the faith of my children. That unadulterated faith. I take the time to see God in all that God created. I take a moment to feel God when a breeze brushes across my cheek. I see God in the magnificence of rainbows. I think about God through the questions of my children. *Does God sneeze? When it's lightning, could God be bowling a strike or taking a picture with a flash?*

I understand that there is more to God than this, but right now, I need this. This childlike faith. These conversations with God are refreshing. They are healing. They are the exact opposite of the weighty, thick, hard-to-swallow notions about God that many adults have who are being strangled with bad theology and suffocating from the trappings of institutionalized religion. That was me. I prayed like that. I preached like that. I believed like that. I breathed like that.

And when God and God's folks hurt me, I broke because of that.

Human error led to church terror, but each day—through the faith of my children and a therapist who reminds me that God is a God of love—I am healing my broken relationship with God. Pray for a sista.

Dear Fellow Survivor . . .

It sucks. Human error turning into church terror is real. The best way that I can describe it is that the trauma becomes like a magnet, and everyone and everything associated with it gets stuck to it. A church leader sexually assaulted you? The church gets drawn in. God gets drawn into the magnetized source of pain. Church folks are drawn into the fold. Scripture? Attracted to the trauma. Preaching and singing and dancing and any other form of praise? Unable to avoid the magnetized pull of my sexual trauma. Everything is drawn into the source of my pain.

God becomes associated with the trauma because God is the one we trust to protect us. God is the one to whom we pray for help in our time of trouble. God is the one we may have cried to *during* our time of trauma, and yet . . . it still happened.

The irony of it all is that everything that gets pulled into the magnetic field of our pain is also that which we seek to repel. We want no part of our trauma. We wish we had not experienced it. We want no part of God. We want no part of the church. We do not want to hear Scripture. We do not want to sing praises. *Praises? Praises?!* For what? Why?

Perhaps, like me, you need to unlearn bad theology. Perhaps you also were taught—or at least gleaned from growing up in the church—that one does not trouble the waters. That church is a place for worshiping God. That there is no room and no place for that which is profane. That no one would believe a church leader could do such disgusting, unwanted things.

Church is not where ugliness resides. It is where God lives. It is not the place where one goes to tell the dirty, unwanted things someone—someone that God has chosen to represent God, no less—has done to you. Plus, who would believe me instead of God's servant? They preach. They serve communion. They have been a member of the church for longer than you've been alive.

They were living their best spiritual life (*insert sarcasm here*). At least that is what they presented. Meanwhile, we are suffering.

Choking on church.

That is me. Can you relate?

I understand if you do not want to attend Bible study, especially with a church leader who was not there for you when you "sounded the alarm." Are they all hypocrites? I understand why you would say, "Yes!" I totally get why you would not want to hear what they have to say about God on Sunday mornings. Not only do you not trust the church leader, but also the subject matter: God. You may be thinking, *What's the point?*

I think back to one of my favorite movies, *The Matrix,* except the context is the church. I wonder whether I would choose the red pill or the blue pill. The fact of the matter is that the choice was never given to me. I had no idea that I had already swallowed the blue pill—the one that helps us to see everything perfect and pure and right and good. Up until I remembered the details of my sexual assault, God was alright with me. Sure, we had some bumps in the road, such as the deaths of immediate family members that rocked me to the core, but that was not God's fault. That was life happening. God helped me through those times.

On that day when my memories returned about my sexual trauma, I felt as if I had unknowingly swallowed the red pill. I knew right then that the life I thought I was living was an illusion. All was *not* right in my world. Life was harsh. The brutal truth was that reality was not filled with unending tranquility. I was blissfully ignorant. Now, I was miserably aware. All too aware. Perhaps you felt or feel the same.

If you are a believer, has your faith wavered because of, or since, your sexual trauma? Did it completely go away? Were you angry with God? Are you still? Please feel what you feel. God knows how we really feel anyway. God knows that we felt abandoned by God. God knows that we are struggling with our relationship with God. We might as well be honest about it.

And while I want to tell you to continue to go to church

and try your best to maintain your faith practices, I cannot. I cannot tell you this because I did not do that. Yes, my assailant was a leader at my church; however, I think I would still have walked away from the church and God even if that were not the case.

What in the world had I believed? Has your sexual trauma caused you to question God? Have you chuckled when you heard someone talk about how good God is? Did you sneeze "bullcrap" when someone was testifying how God was there for them? Did it bother you because you feel that God was not there for you when you needed God?

I understand. And after five-plus years of therapy, I am at the point when I am willing to *consider* giving God a try again. *And I am an ordained minister! And I teach at a seminary!* And I share this with my students the same way I am sharing this with you. And you know what? They appreciate it. They appreciate that I do not hide the fact that I struggle with my faith. That I struggle with the notion of theodicy: Why do bad things happen to good people? They nod their head in agreement when I say that there are times when I do not want to hear about God or read the Word of God.

I am human. I am an embodiment of flesh and blood struggling to make my way through this thing called life the best way I can. I may get weak at times, but I am resilient. I continue to do the work to get back to whatever kind of "normalcy" there is for me, hesitantly reaching out for God along the way. Perhaps this is you.

Breathe deeply. It is not a race. There is no time limit. (*Do not let anyone tell you that you better get right with God right now!*) God knows your heart. I truly believe that. God knows when we will come around, even when we do not know ourselves. God knows that the little bud that remains from a wild and audacious faith will eventually flourish again.

It is a journey. Be gentle with yourself.

It has not been easy for me. It may not be easy for you, and that is okay. It is hard trusting again—even if it is with your higher power. We have been wounded. We have felt abandoned. We have felt betrayed. God knows this. Do you think God does not know how you feel? God does. And I have to believe that God will be with us as we seek to love God again more fully. I *must*.

I have to believe that God is more than what those church leaders told me, and God definitely has to be more than what they showed me. As I type this, I am praying that God will tell me what God wants me to say to you—to myself. This is so hard! I am nowhere near where I want to be with God. I am not as trusting . . . but, oh, I want to be.

So what does healing a broken relationship with God look like? I can only tell you what it looks like for me. For me, it entails starting over. It includes going back to the basics. Of the beauty of God in nature. Of seeing God in the love I receive from my husband, mother, and children.

It includes letting go of the pressure and consequence-ridden, faith-based religiosity—*do this for God, or God will punish you*—that I have been taught, and embracing a childlike spirituality. It means trying to be "in awe" of God again. Seeing

God in the little things, like the way a bunny hops through the grass as it traverses my backyard.

It means being determined to be okay with not sitting in the pew every Sunday, knowing that God is not keeping attendance. It means distancing God from institutionalized religion. It involves having small conversations with God: *Hi God. I need you. Help me.* It necessitates lots and lots of grace and gentleness that I bestow upon myself when my efforts to commune with God are frustrated or seem forced or rote.

Healing my relationship with God includes laughter. Fun. Silliness. As I note in chapter 12, real joy *really is real* . . . even in the midst of surviving. Healing my relationship with God also includes a lack of structure. It involves thinking about God on my own terms. In my own ways. Without allowing anyone to impose their view of how my relationship with God should be. I am done with that.

And I am realizing the more I commune with God in this way, separate and distinct from liturgical practices, memorized creeds, and particularized ecclesial and denominational rules and traditions, the more I am able to remove those layers that separate me from the loving God within. I need to distance myself from these things because this is what my assailant and the people to whom I "sounded the alarm" represent. I have not yet distinguished them from God.

Healing one's relationship with God is a process. There is both progression and regression. And that is okay. Eventually, you will find yourself having moments with God that please your soul and bring a smile to your face. And all you can say is, "Wow."

I want us, fellow survivors, to learn to separate the divine from the profane. My hope for us is that we will be able to trust God again. I would love for us to be able to see church leaders as the sinful beings that they are, because *we all are*. And just because they stand before us at the pulpit or sit in the pews on Sunday, it does NOT mean that God has approved everything they do or say. Heck, some of them were not even called by God; they called themselves! Lord, help!

My prayer for each of us is that we will first love ourselves. Love who we are *despite* . . . Love what we see in the mirror *even in the face of* . . . Love who we are now, even though we have changed *since* . . . Love who we will become *although* . . . Love ourselves just the way we are *even with* . . . *regardless of* . . .

My prayer is that God will reach us where we are. That God will be patient with us. That God will hold us even when we want to push God away. That God will love on us even when we shun God. That God will enter our hearts even when we try our darnedest to shut God out.

I pray that God will bring folks into our lives who will feed our souls, who will help us to pick and toss out the weeds of bad theology and even horrible church folk, help plant within us a message that God is love, and surround us with people who strive to be agents of God's love.

Lord, help me as I write this! I am struggling because what I want for each of us is that which I have not yet attained.

And yet I cannot give up! I am leaning on the faith of my mother and grandmother here. I still do not know how my mother continues to say, "Yes, X happened, *but God is good.*" I just do not get it, but oh how I envy it.

Help us, oh God.

Help us to see you in the midst of these murky, stinking waters. Help us to feel you instead of the touches we do not want and wish we never felt. Help us to hear your voice instead of the utterances of our assailant or the statements of rejection by those we sought aid from. Renew us, oh God. Help us to believe in you and your steadfast love again.

Help us on our journey to believe.

To believe in us.

To believe in you.

To be . . .

Dear Caregiver . . .

Do not push us. Do not beat us over the head with Scripture. It will not have the effect you desire. The exact opposite may happen, actually. (If you have not read chap. 10, please do so.) Do not suggest we get baptized again (if one's tradition allows it). Do not suggest we read the Bible more or pray more.

Be willing to meet with us at a place of our choosing since the church may serve as a reminder of our trauma, or of our troubled relationship with God. The church can be a place of trauma. Furthermore, not all healing happens within its walls.

And by all means, avoid making judgments. A survivor of

sexual assault who wants nothing to do with God is not weak. They are not backsliding. They are not heathens. They. Are. Hurting. Tell them that the faith they had *before* their assault may not be the same as it is *after* their assault, and that is okay.

Trauma has changed them. And perhaps what they need from God has changed. Their views about God have been altered. Life for them will never be the same, so why would one expect their relationship with God to remain the way it used to be?

Do not pressure us. We may not be interested in restorative justice. We may not want to hear that justice belongs to God. You may be trained to hold space for the survivor to confront the abuser, but we may not be ready for that. We may not want that at all! Ask questions, and then listen to us.

Know that the effects of sexual assault can last a long while, if not forever. Our bodies may have healed physically, but the scars (mental and spiritual) are still there. When we shut our eyes, we can see and feel things being inflicted over and over again. There are daily reminders of our trauma. We can be triggered by a horrific retelling of someone else's trauma or simply be reminded by not wanting to be touched by an intern at a doctor's office.

With each reminder, we dust ourselves off and start the process of healing all over again. The same is true for spiritual healing. Let us set the pace. Let the process of reimagining and redefining the divine and our relationship to God happen as the survivor sees fit. Not according to what you deem appropriate.

Nevertheless, be patient with us. Do not give up on us.

As survivors, we are hurting. We are hurting because we do not know why we had to experience such unbearable trauma. We are hurting because we feel as if God abandoned us. We are hurting because church leaders, who are supposed to be God's representatives, did not support us. In some cases, it was the church leader who sexually assaulted us.

Know that we do not have to sit in a pew to worship God. Know that the church is often a place of terror. Know that our presence within those walls may harm us more than do us any good. Know that we are struggling with our faith, and for good reason.

Realize that the trauma a sexual abuse survivor *of faith* endures may lead to a *broken* relationship with God.

What we want is justice. What we want is to see our assailant arrested, removed from their ecclesial leadership position (if they have one), and be exposed for the vile, disgusting person that they are!

We want justice. Not Jesus. *Unless Jesus comes wielding a sword.* We want the satisfaction of revenge. Not the sacredness of rituals. We want our assailant violated. Not sermons saying that vengeance belongs to God. We want them vulnerable. Not refrains of "victory being mine," because it isn't . . . *yet*. We want them exposed. Not an exposé of how we are "covered" with the blood of Jesus.

Even though.

Even though it may not fix it or us. It still may not be enough.

Do not question our feelings. Do not reprimand us. Do not present yourself as holier than thou. You have not gone through what we went through. Even if you are also a survivor, our experiences are different. We are different. We deal with trauma differently. Our relationships with God—if we had them before our sexual trauma—are different.

We relied on God to protect us. We trusted God and God's Word to help us and deliver us from our time of trouble. We do not want to hear about Jesus's suffering. We do not want to hear, "Why not you?" And for God's sake, do not tell us that Jesus himself said, "In this world you will have trouble. But take heart! I have overcome the world" (John 16:33 NIV).

That does not help us! Obviously, we already know this since we have experienced trouble! We know that we were not promised safety at all times, but it does not help us to be reminded of that.

What we need from you is understanding. Patience. Gentleness. We need you to remember that we are human—just as you are. We may need you to sit with us in our pain, in our doubts, in our discomfort. We need you to simply listen when we talk about our disappointment in God. We do not want a sermon or a lecture. We need you to hear our cries, hear our anger, hear our frustration with all things church and all things God-related.

We need to know that no matter what we feel or say, we are accepted. We need to hear that no matter how far we are from God right now that God will still be there when we are ready. We need to hear that although we cannot feel God's presence—and we surely did not feel God during our sexual assault—that God has not left us. We may say, *"Yeah right"* at the time, but it gets in there. Eventually.

We need a sounding board. We may need to go old-school and pull out a paper and a pen and create two columns: God vs. church folks. We may need to literally write out the qualities of God and that of human beings despite the religious trappings that clergy may don. We need you to help us clear the murky waters that make it hard for us to see God for God's own self.

We may need you to just hold our hand as we struggle with our faith. By all means, pray for us on your own. We may even answer in the affirmative if you ask to pray with us. We may also say, "No thanks." Be okay with that.

I do not believe that God will give up on us. Your job is not to "save our souls" by splashing us with holy water, adding us to the public prayer list without our permission, forcing us to listen to you cite Scripture, or shoving videos or clips of sermons in our faces.

We came to you because we need someone to walk this journey with us. We are struggling with our faith. We are struggling with what we *thought* we knew about God. We are wrestling with the knowledge that God is all-powerful and yet seemed powerless when we were being sexually assaulted.

We need comfort. We need care. We need someone to listen to us. Validate our truths. Comfort us. Be with us. And when we are ready, walk with us as we take baby steps to journey back to God. To gently push us forward as we take two steps forward and one step back when we consider trusting God again. To pay attention to us and notice when we need to take a break or a detour on our journey of faith.

Follow our lead. If we move slowly, move slowly. If we take quick steps, move faster. If we request that at times you take over, then do so, all the while considering how the pace affects us. We are on a journey together, but never forget that we invited you on this ride. Respect that.

And as we journey together, if you are of the praying kind, pray that eventually the human error that led to our church terror will no longer frustrate, hinder, or prevent the love for God we once had. Pray that the love between God and us will again be one that is beautiful, growing, and maturing.

Just. Pray.

15

Journeying Together toward Your Own Form of Healing

My journey throughout these years after having "sounded the alarm" has been a bumpy one. I imagine that I suffered alone until my brain saved me from my sexual trauma by hiding it somewhere in the recesses of my mind. I had not told anyone what had happened to me at that time.

As you have read, the people to whom I told my truth were either not ready, did not have the tools and expertise, or were not interested in helping me. Except my husband and mother. They provided exactly what I needed: care, comfort, acceptance, and a hand to hold along the journey. They also encouraged me to set up an appointment with my therapist as soon as possible.

My therapist continues to walk with me as I take one moment at a time (a day at a time is too intimidating at times) in this thing called life. I talk about a journey toward your own form of healing because I am uncertain of the final destination.

I do not know what healing looks like for me. Is it a complete erasure of my sexual trauma? I do not think I will ever forget the parts that I do remember. Is it freedom from being triggered, or having a quick "bounce back" time once I am triggered?

Does healing entail bringing my assailant to justice? Does it mean that he is finally punished for what he did to me? Would him getting a tarnished record wipe my stained slate clean? While seeing him get what he deserved would feel good (*I must be honest here*), it still will not remove the dirt that he left behind on my *then* untarnished–because–permission–was–granted body.

Healing is a journey. A long, difficult, and at times fulfilling one. Because I tend to put too much pressure on myself to complete personal goals, it is helpful for me to see my journey as one without a destination. As I mentioned earlier, I do not know what that destination is. Thus I have decided to just enjoy it. There may be rocks to traverse along the way, scraping my feet. I may trip and fall, but I know that I am not alone. My husband is there, my mother is there, and my therapist is a phone call away.

My journey toward healing includes having moments where I can genuinely smile. It is being fully present with my children and experiencing in awe at the wonder they have toward life. Healing to me means following a mentor's advice to put an hourly reminder in my phone to tell me to *breathe deeply.* You would be surprised how often our breathing is short and choppy. Breathing deeply has been a great help to my well-being.

Journeying together means having someone you trust to hold your hand and gently tug you along the way when you get stuck and are afraid to move along. *I am right here with you.* Having a partner on the journey means having someone sit on the side of the road with you as you fall apart, with a tissue or an adult beverage or your favorite sweet at the ready. They have your back with no judgment and with the utmost care and sensitivity.

I guess you can call my form of healing taking care of my well-being. Being gentle with myself. Loving on myself. Taking the time to understand who I am *now.* Learning to be my own advocate. Speaking my truth without concern for whether I will be believed. That is something that I continue to work on, especially since I decided to publish my truth. Yikes!

And yet here I am. Doing just that. And I feel good. I have a handful of folks who have been with me throughout the entire process of remembering, reliving, scrutinizing, analyzing, and writing my trauma. These wonderful sister-colleagues of mine became essential and life-saving to me on this journey because as I purged my soul onto these pages, they took them from me. They took my truth and provided feedback in the form of probing questions that did not lead to self-doubt but rather helped me to tell my truth with more clarity. They saved me from having to relive this now-written trauma by proofreading and editing it for me. *You know who you are. I love you.*

What I found to be a welcome surprise was that writing this book also helped me to meet new survivors as they travel on their own journey. Do you know how many people are intrigued by seeing an African American woman typing away at her computer with facial expressions of pain and threatening tears? Lots. And about half of those people who inquire what I am working on are survivors themselves. We briefly speak, gently walking on each other's journey and avoiding potential landmines. They depart with well wishes and prayers.

I am on my journey. *I am on my journey!* I have been trapped in an emotional vortex of anger and pain that made it difficult for me to see how I could possibly begin to move on from it. Nevertheless, here I am. The love of my husband, mother, and sons has made my journey easier. Better. Pleasant and fun.

My therapist (*God bless you!*) has made my journey a life-long lesson on self-love. She has made me fall in love with myself. I have learned to be gentle with myself. *"You have to stop should'n all over yourself, Shanell. 'I should be doing this. I should be doing that.' STOP! God created us to be human BEings, not human DOings."* Sitting still, simply *being*, made me antsy. I could not handle the way my mind wandered to places I did not want it to go. I needed to keep busy. I am not as anxious about being alone with my thoughts anymore. I am not *as* anxious.

On this, my journey toward healing, I have learned how to take better care of myself when I am triggered. I go through an intentional thinking process, something along the lines of *he-was-in-the-wrong, it-was-not-my-fault, you-are-safe-now,* and the like. It works for me *most of the time.* Those other times when I cannot handle it, when the record of my sexual trauma is stuck on repeat and those feelings of self-doubt creep in, I call on those who have committed themselves to helping me progress along my journey. And if what they say or do does not immediately help, I feel better knowing that I am not suffering alone.

I do not have to journey alone. My journey toward healing is a moment-by-moment process. Healing is not the destination. Healing is happening with each good moment I have. Healing occurs when I am able to push through a flashback. Healing is happening as I breathe. I am healing. I do not know what healing looks like to you, but my prayer and hope is that you do not have to go on your journey alone.

Journey together.

Dear Fellow Survivor . . .

Breathe deeply. Do it again.

It is hard. You may not be ready. You may not be able to fathom the notion of healing. You may want it, but you have no idea if it is possible to attain. You may even laugh maniacally at anyone who suggests it is. I know I did. *Yeah right! Get out of my face with that . . . !*

You may still wake up in a cold sweat from a nightmare.

You may be afraid or hesitant to leave your home or go to church, for that matter, because . . . The marks may fade and go away, but you can see them. You can still feel them being inflicted. You may, right now, be wallowing in self-doubt and blame. You may be sitting in darkness (even though you sit in a well-lit room). Whatever you may be experiencing at this moment, I am so sorry. It sucks. I wish I could be there for you. But please . . .

Seek out a friend and/or professional to sit with you in your pain until you are ready to begin your journey toward whatever healing looks like for you. Everyone's journey is different. Do not compare what you might need to the needs of others. Focus on you.

Let me repeat: Find *and* go see a therapist. I put emphasis on actually making an appointment *and going* to it. This is because we may have found a therapist, or someone may have put the name and phone number of a professional in our hands, or the contact information for someone may have been Airdropped into our phones, but if you do not call, set up the appointment, and go . . .

This is why it helps to have someone to journey along with you. They can dial the number for you and stand there while you make the appointment. Share your calendars, and I bet the partner on your journey may even take you at the scheduled time.

I am not going to say that we cannot journey alone; perhaps you can. I could not. I needed people. It made my journey that much more doable, especially during the difficult times. Having someone to walk through this process with you is advantageous because they can help hold you accountable. *Are you taking care of yourself? Have you eaten? When is your next appointment? Hang up, set it up, and then call me right back.*

It also helps to have someone assist you in determining what you need. Some of the questions they might ask are: *What does healing look like to you? Why this and not that? What do you need from me to help you achieve that? I like how you are thinking, but I think you are setting yourself up for failure with something that huge. Plus, if you break that goal into smaller parts, you will have more reasons and times to celebrate! And I can be with you every step of the way.*

It is okay to not know what you need! You may not be able to see your hand before your face right now. You may not be able to formulate a thought right now. What I want you to know is that a journey toward healing can involve anything that is positive, healthy, and life-giving to you. It can be in the form of retaining a lawyer, doing yoga, creating various forms of art, meditation, going to a retreat center, and the like. Reengage your senses, and take care of yourself. No one can judge you on what makes you feel good!

Think about what you need from the person with whom you will journey. If they are a fellow survivor, make sure that each of you benefits, and one person is not monopolizing the other person's time and exhausting their emotional reserve. You may consider having conversations with each other about what healing means to each of you, write them down, and then share them. Talk about them without judgment and without comparison. Ask each other how you can help one another achieve their goals in a way that it does not take away what you each need to do and be for yourself.

Do not sacrifice yourself and your needs. If you find that journeying with a fellow survivor does not work for you, say it. It is imperative that you be your own advocate. You may recall the conversation I mentioned earlier with a woman who was also a survivor who shared her experience with sexual trauma in a tit-for-tat fashion in an attempt to one-up me. After that conversation, she suggested that we stay in touch in order to be there for each other. I told her something to the effect of: *I appreciate the offer; however, I need to respectfully decline.* That is it. No further explanation required. If a person pushes back, just say, "It's how I feel," and move on.

Take care of yourself. You do not have the luxury of helping someone along their journey at the expense of your own! Be gentle with yourself. Your needs come first. Dealing with your own pain is your first priority. Seeking help so that you can sleep at night should be number one on your list. If the person you choose is also a survivor, it may help that they have already made healthy progress on their own path toward healing and thus can function as more of a guide.

You may not know if the partner you choose is a fellow survivor until you speak your truth. If only you can go up to someone and say, *"Hey! Are you a survivor of sexual trauma? I am trying to find someone to walk with me on my journey toward healing."* Wishful thinking. Even after you share your truth, whoever you tell may still keep their truth close to their chest. They may not tell you. Ever. They may not be ready to "sound the alarm." They may be embarrassed or ashamed or riddled with self-doubt. They may not *remember* their trauma until something you say triggers their own. Whatever the reasons, what I want you to know is that it is important to be aware and observant about your relationship. Make sure you are getting as much from the person with whom you walk along your journey as they are. They should get (professional) help for themselves as well.

The same applies if the person you seek is not a fellow survivor. Make sure your boundaries are respected. Do they allow you to set the pace, and only nudge you in healthy ways? Do they listen to what you have to say? Do they validate what you say, or are they judgmental and skeptical? Are you being taken care of in a way that is comfortable for you? Do they respect your personal space if you have made it known? Do they try to force you to do something that you do not want to do? Do they make you feel bad if you have a setback? Do they make fun of you for having nightmares even though some time has passed since your sexual trauma occurred? Pay attention to your needs and make sure they are met. If not, move on!

I am not an expert, but journeying with someone has proven beneficial to me. I am simply sharing with you my experience, namely, what did and did not work *for me*. You have to figure out what works for you. YOU. You may not know what you need at the moment, but that is precisely why you may want someone to be with you along the way. Talk about what you (think you might) need.

JOURNEY TOGETHER with someone. Cry together. Laugh together. Learn together. In whatever form it takes, HEAL. TOGETHER.

Dear Caregiver . . .

Breathe deeply. Do it again.

You may have been caught off guard. You may have had no idea that you would be the person a survivor of sexual trauma would turn to for help.

You have an opportunity to be a source of comfort and companionship for someone who has a long, tough, but rewarding journey ahead of them.

Decide. Decide sooner rather than later if you want to function in that capacity. You do not need to be a professional, but you should know how to locate and contact one in case a survivor needs it. You do not need to know what to say. Listen, and then ask the survivor what they need.

Be gentle with them, and make sure that they are gentle with themselves as well. Provide comfort without judgment. Praise the baby steps of progress that they have made, even if it is getting through an hour without (*insert whatever is challenging for them here*). Allow them to cry until their reserve runs out, and sit with them while it replenishes, and then when the tears form and overflow again. JUST BE THERE.

If you are a survivor yourself and you have not dealt with your own pain and trauma, you may not be the best person for this task. (See chap. 7.) BE UPFRONT. If you are unable to be a source of comfort for another survivor—even if you do not want to share your reasons why—tell them that (in the best way you know how). Wish them the best, and then seriously consider getting professional help for yourself. Seek the care YOU need.

If you are a fellow survivor and have gone or are going through therapy, you may find comfort in walking along a journey toward healing with a fellow survivor. Talking about your trauma in a way that does not retrigger each other may help releasing it from within you—at least little by little. Hearing someone else boldly talk about being a survivor, and how what they went through was not their fault (no matter what anyone says), may help chip away your own self-doubt and give you the courage to claim and state your own truth. Rise up! (*Read the above section to Fellow Survivors.*)

Journeying together means that you have decided to be a companion to a survivor on their journey toward healing. They may or may not know what form their healing will take. You may be asked to be present with them as they "sound the alarm." You may actually *be that person* to whom they tell their truth.

GATHER RESOURCES. You may not have them on-hand at the time of your encounter, but it is never too late to find them. Do you know the contact information for a good therapist and/or the local sexual assault crisis center? Do you know your church's sexual assault policy? Do you have one? If so, enforce it! I do not pretend to know what that entails. If both the survivor and their assailant belong to the same church, there may be certain protocols to follow. Whatever they are, do it, all the while validating the truth of the survivor. What they told *is their truth* no matter what the assailant says. Honor that.

Are you a mandated reporter? Then follow protocol.

Journeying together is an emotional process. Know what you can and cannot handle. Be honest and transparent. Know when you have reached your limit in terms of providing care, or in terms of the amount of emotional drain you can tolerate. Pay attention to your own needs as you take care of those of a survivor. It is of no benefit to anyone if you fall apart while helping to keep a survivor together. Be gentle with yourself as well.

Saying yes to a survivor who has requested that you be with them as they journey toward their form of healing is not a stress-free or even a comfortable experience, but it can be a rewarding one. Learn *with* each other. Grow *with* each other. A survivor may need you to comfort them during this time, but it does not mean that we are weak. We just need someone to be with us as we get stronger. We may seem fragile, but we will not break. We may be going through some difficult times, but that does not mean that we do not have anything to offer you. Our sexual trauma is not all we are. We are people who have experienced something that changed the course of our life, but it did not end it. WE ARE SURVIVORS! In the midst of journeying with us, you may learn something about perseverance and strength.

Thank you for journeying with us!

16

Strength for the Journey

This was not easy. My journey with writing this book took a lot out of me. I was mentally exhausted and emotionally drained. I experienced a wide range of negative emotions, from deep sadness and melancholy to extreme bouts of intense anger and rage. So yeah, reliving my sexual trauma depleted me, but thinking about the folks who journeyed with me along the way and the progress I made over time with my therapist while writing this book also gave me life. I am proud of myself! As I said in the previous chapter, healing, for me, is not an end goal. I do not even know what that would look like. Healing is breathing. Healing happens moment by moment in the most simple way: loving myself.

So as I sit here writing this chapter, I am smiling. I did it! I faced my sexual trauma head-on, oftentimes shaking in my boots. Afraid that I would "go under" into a deep depression and struggle getting out. I did not want to face the self-doubt that I felt and sometimes still feel. It is so discouraging and embarrassing. As I reflected on my experience, I did not want to see his face on Sunday mornings like I used to, but I did. I did not want to witness myself sharing a laugh with him or feeling loved under his praise, but I did. I hated it, but I also know that I blossomed from it *then*. It was so hard reliving the encounters I had with folks I thought would choose me and be there for me. Folks I loved and would do anything for. Sacrificed for. Sacrificed *myself* and my joy for. It was hard hearing the harsh things they said and experiencing all over again the betrayal, rejection, and lack of concern for my well-being. It shattered me, and it rocked my faith in those I loved. It made me question all of my relationships. Love does not equal loyalty. Does it? *Did they love me?*

I feel as if I have just completed an intense, extremely long, and very public therapy session. Talk about being vulnerable. The interesting thing is that while being vulnerable is uncomfortable and quite humbling, it comes quite naturally to me. I am vulnerable in the classroom and in the pulpit. I do not *intend* to be this way; it just happens.

So writing this book does not come as a surprise. Twenty-plus years after my sexual trauma, I "sounded the alarm," and five years after that, I was still struggling with everything I wrote in this book. I did not think that I would be over it by then, but my wounds were still inflamed and tender with no signs of getting better. This was because I did not want to face my trauma. I tried to bury my feelings. I pretended that I was okay. It looked like I had everything together. But I was broken. I was fractured within. And that was a dangerous place to be. It was time to face the music, as they say. So I began to journal. I began to write what I remembered. I jotted down how I felt, how I *still* feel. I wrote, and I wrote. As my therapist says, "I am doing the work."

That is what *touched* is. What you have read is the written version of how I am doing the work. How I am journeying toward my healing. Experiencing and growing from the pain. Crying and laughing, sometimes at the same time. Shaking my head at myself in disappointment and nodding my head at myself in praise and approval. This is me. What you get is me. The unadulterated version of me, I give to you. It is *my* experience, *my* analysis of *my* sexual trauma, and *my* unsolicited advice based on how I felt and what I needed yet did not receive. It is important to remember that I am not an expert, nor do I claim to be.

Dear Fellow Survivor . . .

YOU ARE LOVED. If no one has said this to you, and you do not think that you are, know that I do. And that matters because I am a dope! (*I hope you are smiling.*) In all seriousness, I do love you because you matter. Your life matters. You are not your trauma! This does not mean that your trauma has not changed you or affected you in any way, such that you can operate as if it never happened. When I say, "You are not your trauma," I mean that there is more to you. What you experienced is only one aspect of your life. It may be a *huge* aspect of your life, especially if you have not gotten help with dealing with it, but it is not everything. There is the rest of you. You are a magnificent, complex individual. There is no one like you. Each of us is unique and has something to offer the world. We need you. You are important. You are loved!

If you have not done so already, find a therapist. Seek a professional who can help you deal with, unpack, and live despite your sexual trauma. I do not think we can do it alone. Find someone who knows what they are doing. They should not spend most of your session talking about themselves. Trust your instincts. If you do not feel you are getting what you need from them, go to someone else. Going to therapy does not mean that you are weak; it means that you want to stay strong!

My hope is that by sharing my experience, you felt affirmed. My aim is to offer you solidarity. My goal is to encourage you to speak your truth and not to let anyone silence you or cause you to question it. I want to validate your truth. Claim your truth, and hold on to it, no matter what anyone says. No matter how long it took you to tell it. No matter if folks disbelieve it because you were able to S.M.I.L.E. (Simply Making It Look Easy). It is your truth. What you read is mine. And no matter what anyone says who reads this book, I will hold on to it with everything I have got. And if I feel the weight of judgment, if I sense even a little bit of self-doubt creep in, I will not hesitate to grab onto my journey partners' hands, which are always extended, and collectively, I will continue to claim my truth.

I want so much for my experience to aid you in any way that it can. I want you to take from my experience whatever will help you and disregard the rest. Take what you need, and leave what does not work for you. Go back and read the chapters as you need them. I designed the book so that each chapter can stand on its own. Cherry-pick this book.

My desire is that you know your worth. That through my encounters you learn to defend and protect yourself. That you speak up when someone says or does something that offends you, hurts you, or when you just want them to be quiet! (*The hand gesture for "Talk to the hand" still works, even if just to stop an unwanted conversation.*)

Know that you do not have to listen to someone beat you over the head with Scripture. For some people, that will be the only thing they know how to do, since Scripture is an important source of comfort for them. Some may even believe that citing Scripture has healing power. It is not for us to judge. But it is our right to stop them if hearing verses from the Bible (or any sacred text) has a negative impact on us. This can be the case even if the survivor is also a believer. Actually, survivors who believe in God are usually the ones who do not want to hear it. Case in point: me.

It is quite alright to not want to hear Scripture. It is quite alright to be angry with God. Yes, I am an ordained minister, and I just said that. God knows anyway! God also knows that it may be hard for you to attend church or hear about anything church-related. God knows if you are finding it hard to see God as a God of love or to differentiate God from God's people. This is especially true when we understand church leaders—those who preach and teach God's Word—as the representative or voice of God. It is unsettling and confusing, and the lines separating the sacred from the profane get blurred when a church leader's actions are the exact opposite of the words they proclaim. As I noted earlier, a church leader is not just God's representative within the walls of the church. They are God's agent wherever they go, even at the scene where our sexual trauma took place by their hands.

No, you absolutely do not need to be present in church on Sundays, especially if your assailant is there. Protect yourself. When you are ready, slowly ease your way back into conversation with God if you have stopped talking to God. Reimagine what spirituality can mean for you, and indulge in that. I hope you find the God you seek. I hope God grabs a hold of you and never lets you go.

You are loved, fellow survivor! Be gentle with yourself. Be patient with yourself. Setbacks are inevitable, but so is progress! Love on yourself. Determine your own form of healing, and seek it, do it, because you deserve it. Find folks who will support you in doing all these things. It is a journey, not a race. Journey together.

Dear Caregiver ...

THANK YOU! Thank you for being there for my fellow survivor. I know you did not expect to be asked to function in this capacity. No one ever is, unless this is your profession. I understand if you are nervous and anxious that you might make a mistake, or that you may not live up to the expectations of a survivor, but guess what? I am glad you feel this way! This means that you care. It means that you will do your best to show up in the best way you know how. It also means that when you do not know what to do, perhaps you will help find the resources a survivor needs to get the help they need.

My hope is that you will glean from my experience various ways to support a survivor. This book is not exhaustive. What worked for me may not work for someone else. If you are reading this book *with* a survivor or *for* a (potential) survivor, have a conversation to figure out what will work for the both of you. Remember, you are journeying *together*, but the survivor invited you. Behave accordingly.

If a survivor comes to you to "sound the alarm," know that we either trust you and believe that you can support us (*in fact, we are banking on that*), or you are in a position of authority and we are seeking some form of justice. Whatever the reason, know that it takes a lot for a survivor to "sound the alarm" *every time we do it.* We may have to do it multiple times, depending on who we need for particular kinds of support, and unfortunately, when those we go to for support reject us and doubt our truth. (*Off to the next . . .*) It is hard enough for us to relive our sexual trauma by telling it, so make it easy for us. Listen.

Listen. Listen to our truths, and do not interrupt unless you know you are unable, or do not want, to handle the situation, or if you are a fellow survivor who may be triggered. Whatever the reason, please stop a survivor as soon as you know you cannot function in this role. It is just plain courtesy. This can also help us avoid feeling as if we wasted our time and from feeling exposed to someone who did not need to *see*. Because when we tell our truths, you cannot unsee what we say. We would prefer to stay covered.

After hearing a survivor's truth, validate it. Even if you are in a position of power, and you have to hear the side of our assailant, what the survivor told you is their truth. Validate this! Make sure they know that you heard them. They need to know that you believe them. Make sure they know this.

During the encounter, be sure to respect our space. Do not touch this unless we say it is okay. Do not encroach on our space if we sit at a distance. We did it for a reason. We need that space. The last thing we want to feel is overcrowded since we might be suffocating because of our trauma, and because of the anxiety having to "sound the alarm" brings.

Know your own limits. Be clear and transparent with us when you do not know how to help us. If you are a survivor yourself, know the impact of your own experience with sexual trauma on the encounter. Do not project. We are not you. Do not compare. Our trauma is not the same. One-upmanship is not welcomed, but it is a snare in which many fellow survivors get caught. Share only if granted permission to do so. Share only in the form of solidarity.

Think before you speak. Rarely do we know what societal assumptions we have internalized until we have spoken them, even when trying to get more information. *How old were you when it happened? Were you wearing something revealing?* If this happens in your encounter with a survivor, apologize.

If you are a believer, ask if we want you to read Scripture. This is especially the case if a survivor is a believer also. If we say no, accept that. If we say yes, ASK what we may want to hear. Choose wisely if we want you to select one. Some verses can cause harm. Remember that Scripture alone is not enough. Scriptures alone do not heal. Christian band-aids do not stick. They have no lasting effect. They do not hold us when we need comfort. They do not make phone calls to therapists or law officials. We need more. We need you!

Thank you for saying yes to journeying together with us. It may feel that the survivor-caregiver relationship is one-sided, and it may be in the beginning, but eventually it may grow into a symbiotic one. Both of you will benefit from this journey. As you journey together, the bond between the two of you will strengthen. You will learn more about yourself as we learn who we are, and who we want to be post-assault. You will be encouraged by witnessing the sheer amount of perseverance and strength a survivor must have to live from moment to moment and to fight to move forward when triggered. We will cry together. Laugh together. Grow together. We may even yell at each other. And all of that is okay. Because we are doing it *together*. And as you journey with us on our path toward healing, you may just end up finding your own.

★★★

In *touched: For Survivors of Sexual Assault Like Me Who Have Been Hurt by Church Folk and for Those Who Will Care*, I offer you my experience from which to learn. I offer you the validation of your truths. I offer you strength for the journey.

By sharing ME, I am offering you, YOU.